A Confessor's Handbook

D1292261

A CONFESSOR'S HANDBOOK

Revised and Expanded Edition

KURT STASIAK, O.S.B.

Paulist Press
New York/Mahwah, N.J.

Nihil obstat: Daniel J. Mahan, S.T.B., S.T.L.
Censor Librorum

Imprimatur: Most Rev. Daniel M. Buechlein, O.S.B.
Archbishop of Indianapolis
September 15, 2009

Cover design by Joy Taylor
Book design by Lynn Else

Library of Congress Cataloging-in-Publication Data

Stasiak, Kurt, 1952–
  A confessor's handbook / Kurt Stasiak. — Rev. and expanded ed.
      p. cm.
  Includes bibliographical references.
  ISBN 978-0-8091-4675-8 (alk. paper)
  1. Confession—Catholic Church. I. Title.
  BX2265.3.S73 2010
  264´.020862—dc22

                                                            2010017936

Published by Paulist Press
997 Macarthur Boulevard
Mahwah, New Jersey 07430

www.paulistpress.com

Printed and bound in the
United States of America

Table of Contents

Table of Contents

Table of Contents

To Michael
Indeed, a friend in word and in deed.

Foreword to the Revised Edition

It's hard to believe a decade has passed since the first publication of *A Confessor's Handbook*. But the success of this book and the desire for an expanded edition come as no surprise to anyone who has read it. In the last ten years its author has travelled the country giving talks and workshops to priests, and the book has found regular use both as a seminary text and as a continuing education resource for priests.

When I was privileged to write the foreword to the first edition, I was the rector of a seminary and associate professor of moral theology. While I still teach moral theology on a part-time basis, I now write from the perspective of a pastor. I am more convinced than ever of the importance of this book, of its topic, and of the insights offered by its author.

Today, the Church continues to face a crisis in the sacrament of reconciliation. Many of us middle-aged and older Catholics remember the long lines in front of the confessionals of every parish on Saturdays. Whatever the failings of the popular theology and practice of that time, Catholics went to confession. Today, except in special seasons or in exceptional places, lines are generally short. Too many Catholics *never* go to confession. A lot of Catholics seem to have very little understanding of sin, or even a solid sense of sin, a situation that cuts at the very heart of the Christian faith. If there is no sin, no need for confession, then there is no need for a

Savior—and Jesus Christ becomes just a good teacher or an admired wonder-worker in time of truly dire need.

Surely there are many complex reasons for the decline in confessional practice, and an adequate response to the situation should also be multifaceted. But one utterly essential component is ensuring that the sacrament of reconciliation be celebrated in a prudent, prayerful, helpful, and inviting manner. That's easy to say, but hard to do. Certainly, some priests have a particular gift for serving as confessors, just as others may have special gifts for preaching, teaching, or administration. But, specially gifted or not, every priest *is* a confessor and now, more than ever, a priest must be well prepared and disposed to celebrate this important sacrament. Yes, it is important for a priest to be prayerful and thus authentically discerning. Yes, it is important that he have a solid theological background concerning the sacrament and the nature of sin and grace. But it must all come together in a prudent, skilled, and maturely human way—and it must come together in the confessional! To this end, Fr. Kurt Stasiak offers *A Confessor's Handbook* in a revised and expanded edition.

What I said in the foreword to the first edition remains true: the reader will find the *Handbook* to be profoundly pastoral. This book draws richly from the Church's sacramental theology, without being yet another review of the history and theology of the sacrament. It offers thoughtful and practical suggestions, without making any claims of being a "how-to" manual. Priests and seminarians, seminary professors, and catechists preparing people for the celebration of the sacrament will find this book to be an essential resource. Parishioners may also find that the book helps their approach to the sacrament, since a positive experience in confession is encouraged by a penitent's understanding of the priest's role as compassionate listener and healer.

Fr. Kurt Stasiak brings a wealth of experience, education, and gifts to *A Confessor's Handbook*. He holds a doctorate in sacramental theology. He is both a publishing scholar as well as an extremely popular and effective teacher. He is a highly regarded spiritual director to many individuals, as well as a sought-after speaker to parish, diocesan, and other Church groups. He has long experience in seminary formation. Perhaps most important, he is himself a good priest and a frequent confessor. He is certainly a person well qualified to advise seminarians and priests in the worthy practice of the sacrament of reconciliation.

Our journey of ongoing conversion from sin to the life of deepening communion with God in Christ is the path of Christian holiness. The celebration of the sacrament of reconciliation is a powerful and privileged help on this journey. Fr. Kurt Stasiak's *A Confessor's Handbook* is a valuable resource for those who are called to guide, to pastor, and to nurture the people of God in the way of holiness.

Fr. Mark O'Keefe, O.S.B.
Pastor, Saint Mary's Catholic Church, Huntingburg, IN,
Associate Professor of Moral Theology, Saint Meinrad
School of Theology

INTRODUCTION

Celebrating the sacrament of reconciliation is among the most significant of encounters priests have with their parishioners. It is certainly one of the most personal. Many priests would even say it is the most demanding.

Significant, personal, demanding. My experience with this sacrament, which includes thirty years of "hearing" confessions and many more years of "going to confession," bears this out. And I am not alone in this. Every priest I know, when asked to recall the especially significant moments of his ministry, refers almost immediately to his ministry as confessor. These priests will describe their celebrations of the sacrament as among the most intensely personal encounters they have had with their parishioners. One priest put it well: "In the sacrament you see a side of your parishioners most people never see. You see them at their best and you see them when they think they're at their worst. Many times they open themselves to you spiritually, emotionally, and psychologically as they will do to no one else. This sacrament is a personal and intense encounter like no other."

Celebrating the sacrament of reconciliation can be a significant and personal experience for both penitent and priest. And for both penitent and priest, the celebration of the sacrament can be demanding. The demands made upon the penitent need no extensive commentary: humility, courage, determination, and trust are those which come immediately to mind. It is the demands the celebration of the sacrament makes upon the minister—and the opportunities afforded him—that are the concerns of this book.

1

In celebrating this sacrament, perhaps more than in any other exercise of their ministry, priests want to be Christ-like. They want to "put on the mind of Christ," as Saint Paul says, and offer the compassion and understanding Christ offered. In this sacrament above all, priests want to be effective stewards of the Lord's grace. They want to be true "ambassadors of peace."

It is ironic then that, as important as the pastoral practice of this sacrament is, many priests begin their ministry without having received any extensive training in "how to hear confessions." Seminary courses usually concentrate on the historical development of the sacrament and the theological concepts associated with sin, grace, reconciliation, and the like. Sometimes seminarians are required to do one or two "practice confessions" with their professor. Ordinarily, however, an always-too-short academic semester prevents a thorough study—and a thorough *practice*—of the sacramental encounter itself. An oft-heard complaint of the newly ordained is that, while they consider they were educated well in the theology and history of the sacrament, they feel their training in its pastoral practice left something to be desired. As one priest friend, ordained for many years, remarked recently: "What I've learned about hearing confessions I've learned entirely on my own. And that bothers me sometimes. The way I hear a confession is the only part of my priestly ministry that I don't, and really *can't*, get any supervision for or evaluation of."

I am writing this book because I wish it had been written for me. I write with three particular audiences in mind. I am writing, first, for my brother priests. As my priest-friend said, we benefit neither from supervision nor from evaluation in our ministry as confessor. *We can't.* And that is why I write this book. I want to offer my brother priests, be they newly-ordained associates or experienced pastors, an extended reflection on the "practice of the confessional." I want to discuss what can take place—what we might do and how we might do it—as we minister to those who bring their sins, situations, and questions to the sacrament of God's pardon and peace.

I write, second, for the seminarians of our Church. I write, not as one who has all the answers, but as a priest and seminary professor who encourages you to prepare now for your ministry in the confessional by beginning to consider how you might deal with your parishioners as they approach you seeking forgiveness, absolution, advice, and reassurance.

Finally, I write for my colleagues who teach in seminaries and schools of theology. *A Confessor's Handbook* cannot replace the texts that detail the history and theology of the sacrament of reconciliation. As an adjunct to those texts, however, it can be an additional practical resource for your students.

In chapter one I discuss five principles concerning the sacramental encounter between priest and penitent. In chapters two and three I offer suggestions on what might be done and said—and what certainly is to be avoided. In chapter four I address special situations priests encounter in the sacrament: the confessions of children or of brother priests, for example, or of those who confess they are at odds with the Church's teaching on sexual ethics.

Three appendices provide further resources. Appendix I reproduces the 1997 document from the Pontifical Council for the Family, a *Vademecum for Confessors Concerning Some Aspects of the Morality of Conjugal Life*. In Appendix II, I discuss how this book might be used in a seminary course, and how confessions might be "practiced." Appendix III addresses how important it is for us priests to approach the sacrament as penitents as well as in our role as confessors. Appendix III is new to this revised and expanded edition of *A Confessor's*

Handbook. I have also added some ten thousand words (about a forty percent addition to the original text) to the four main chapters, words that reflect ten more years of seminary teaching, presenting workshops and days of recollection to a number of presbyterates and, of course, reflection upon my continuing ministry as confessor.

Priests or seminarians should not consider *A Confessor's Handbook* a recipe book. This book will not tell you exactly what to say or do in every situation—or even in "such-and-such" a situation. Such a book would be as impossible to write as it would be dangerous to follow. This book cannot tell a confessor "what to do." *But it can suggest what he might consider.* It can suggest different ways, perhaps a better way, that each confessor, in his words, with his skills, and from his personality, can minister God's pardon and peace to his parishioners. Many of the suggestions I offer are obvious. They are suggestions I continue to find helpful and effective—reference points to which I often return—when dealing with a variety of people in a variety of situations. I do not claim that what I offer is the best way to hear a confession, and I know that other priests, reflecting upon their experience in the confessional, will disagree with me about specific points. I do not doubt others could offer better examples, more solid insights, or more effective ways of dealing with saints and sinners. So much the better! If further discussion of our ministry in the sacrament is one result of my writing this book, my goal will have been met. My way is not the only way. But it is *a* way— a thoughtful way, a way from *my* experience—that, hopefully, will encourage you to think about *your* way.

Throughout this book I use "preconciliar terms" (*confessor, penitent, hearing confession*) and their "postconciliar counterparts" (*minister, parishioner, celebrating reconciliation*). As a priest and professor, my thinking inclines toward the latter; as a writer, I find that use of the former often allows a welcome economy of words.

Concerning the examples and illustrations in this book, the seal of the confessional is absolutely respected and maintained. None of the examples I offer is open to personal identification. Nor are any of the examples and situations unique to my experience. The incidents I pose and discuss come from many sources: the "practice confessions," "confessional case studies," and discussions that are a regular part of the reconciliation courses I have taught; my thirty years of experience as priest, spiritual director, counselor, and teacher; discussions with colleagues, seminarians, and parishioners; on occasion, my imagination; often, my reflection on questions asked or answers given.

I wish to thank the Rt. Rev. Justin DuVall, O.S.B., archabbot of Saint Meinrad Archabbey, and the Very Rev. Denis Robinson, O.S.B., president-rector of Saint Meinrad Seminary, for allowing me the time and means to prepare this revised and expanded edition of *A Confessor's Handbook*. When he was president-rector of our seminary some years ago, the Most Rev. Daniel M. Buechlein, O.S.B., now archbishop of Indianapolis, taught me the basics of hearing confessions. I benefited from his instruction then, as I benefit now from his continuing encouragement and support. I am grateful also for the continued assistance of my colleague, Fr. Larry Richardt, a priest of the Archdiocese of Indianapolis and, at various times, academic dean, vice rector, and director of spiritual formation at Saint Meinrad Seminary.

I continue to benefit from my students, who always have many questions and, often, some fine answers. In this regard I thank several of my recent students—now ordained confessors themselves—who critiqued a draft of this revised and expanded manuscript: Frs. John Hollowell and Peter Marshall (Archdiocese of Indianapolis), Matthew Long (Diocese of Shreveport), and Gary Mayer (Archdiocese of Dubuque), and my confrere Fr. Christian Raab, O.S.B. I offer a special word of thanks to the Sisters of Charity of Leavenworth, Kansas, who provided me with several weeks of warm shelter, good food, and restful quiet, so that I might work on this edition free from the preoccupations of my usual responsibilities.

I dedicated the original edition of *A Confessor's Handbook* to Monsignor Jerry Neufelder, an experienced priest and a fine friend. I was happy to have had the opportunity to hand the original manuscript to him personally. Tragically, Jerry was killed in a car accident in July 2002. Jerry was instrumental in the formation of hundreds of priests during his years at Saint Meinrad Seminary, and I have no doubt he now intercedes for all priests—new and old—from a place close to God's right hand.

I dedicate this edition of *A Confessor's Handbook* to Fr. Michael Zoellner, O.S.B., a monk and priest of St. Benedict's Abbey, Atchison, Kansas, and currently the chaplain at the Motherhouse of the Sisters of Charity of Leavenworth. I first experienced his encouragement, support, and friendship many years ago. I am humbled, and most grateful, to realize these gifts have lasted much longer than I would have had any reason to expect or right to deserve.

CHAPTER ONE

THE SACRAMENTAL DIALOGUE BETWEEN PRIEST AND PENITENT:

basic principles

Previous generations of Catholics seemed to bring their sins to confession regularly if not eagerly. Today many of our parishioners see no reason to make even seasonal celebration of the sacrament a part of their lives. An extensive study in 1995[1] concluded that only about twenty percent of today's Catholics go to private confession, and more recent studies reflect comparable statistics.[2]

Some argue that communal reconciliation services, attractively arranged and joyfully celebrated, will encourage more people to make greater use of the sacrament. Others recommend more frequent preaching and teaching about the sacrament, with special emphasis on the social and ecclesial aspects of sin and forgiveness. There are those who advocate General Absolution as the form of reconciliation the Church should adopt as its ordinary practice. And occasionally we come across a brother priest who maintains that the fire and brim-stone approach remains the best solution.

Whatever the suggestions for the present or the recommendations for the future, one thing is clear. What contributes most to the significance of the sacrament in the lives of our parishioners is not the aesthetically or emotionally-arranged atmosphere. Nor is it the music, however carefully selected and performed, or the catechesis or homily, however well prepared and delivered. To be sure, all of these elements are important, for they contribute to an effective, meaningful celebration. In addition to the power of God's grace, however, the single most important factor, the *determining* factor in the celebration of the sacrament, is what takes place in those moments of personal encounter between the priest and his parishioner. People will respond to—will indeed be impressed by—what happens *around* them. But for most, the "make-it-or-break-it" factor will be what happens *to* them.

The implication for our ministry is clear. When we priests gather with our parishioners to celebrate the Eucharist, we want to be more than liturgical functionaries. We want to do more than enter, perform the ritual, and depart. The same holds for our ministry as confessors. If the sacrament is to be an effective means of conversion for our parishioners, its effectiveness is in no small way dependent upon our approach to, our dynamic ministering of, the sacrament. In other words, the sacrament will be a more effective element of conversion in the lives of our parishioners to the degree that we consider our ministry as confessors as allowing us the opportunity to be more than "hearers, penancers, and absolvers."

Gerard Broccolo has described the power of the sacrament of reconciliation as "quiet dynamite." Writing shortly after the *Rite of Penance* was revised by the conciliar reforms, he commented that "The small handful of confessors who have allowed themselves to respond to the challenge of the Spirit, in allowing this Sacrament to come alive as an overwhelming 'event' in the lives of their penitents, promise an exciting breath of fresh air in the immediate future of the Church."[3] There are some (on both sides of the screen) who question the value and effectiveness of sacramental reconciliation in the lives of individuals and that of the Church at large. I share Broccolo's conviction, however. Because of God's merciful grace, the sacrament of reconciliation is "quiet dynamite." It can change lives. It does establish our parishioners and our Church more fully in God's grace. It can help priests and penitents alike to become instruments of God's peace to one another.

But the sacrament does not do this automatically or magically. To continue with the image of "quiet dynamite," the fuse still needs to be lit for the power of this sacramental reconciliation to explode in the hearts of our people. The sacrament of reconciliation is founded upon, effects, and expresses the power of *God* working through us—God, "whose power working in us can do more than we can ask or imagine" (Eph 3:20). But it is we ministers who have the best opportunity to light the fuse that unleashes the power of God's word of pardon and peace within the hearts of our people.

What is in fact unique to the celebration of sacramental reconciliation is that the opportunity and the challenge for personal investment in the sacrament far exceed that which can be realized in other sacramental encounters. In no other sacrament do either priests or parishioners have the opportunity to participate with the depth and intensity possible in the sacrament of reconciliation. In no other sacrament will either priest or penitent reveal who they are, what they think, and what they seek, as they are able to do in the sacrament of reconciliation.

What makes these moments beautiful—and demanding—is that they are not scripted. One cannot prepare to hear a confession in the same way one prepares a homily or a catechesis. It is true that the sacrament is "effective" (in the Scholastic sense) when sins are confessed, contrition is present, absolution is given, and the penance is performed. But while this bare minimum suffices for sacramental validity, many parishioners approach the sacrament seeking something more than the precise, exact following of the ritual.

In this chapter I propose five principles concerning the nature and the importance of what I call the "sacramental dialogue," the "conversation in the confessional" between priest and parishioner. To call this conversation a "dialogue" is not to imply it is simply conversation. The primary purpose of this conversation *is that it be sacramental.* At its best the sacramental dialogue is a "door opener": it allows, encourages, and promotes a tangible experience of God's forgiveness and so is a true and powerful instrument of grace. The five principles I discuss here underlie the suggestions I offer in the following chapters.

A FIRST PRINCIPLE: An encounter with Christ, his Church, and his minister

Sacraments are encounters with Christ and his Church. The extent to which the sacrament of reconciliation can be a fruitful encounter with the Christ who is our peace and our hope—the extent to which the penitent is invited to meet and be touched by Christ—is in large part up to us.

Hopefully, the days of "sacramental magic" are over. Today we emphasize that these liturgical actions are not isolated moments in time, a kind of "sacred parenthesis" in the lives of Christians having little if anything to do with the way life is really lived in the world. The sacraments are defining moments for Christians—and for the world. They remind us who we are, in whom we believe, in whose name we were baptized, and whose footsteps we follow. The sacraments challenge us to remember that, should the world want to know what we Christians believe, they have every right to look first at what we do. As the theologian Hans Urs von Balthasar once remarked, "The value of Christianity need not be seen in itself; but it must be seen *in us.*"

If "going to confession" is to be experienced by our people as a grace-filled sacramental encounter with Christ, a wise and effective dialogue within the context of the sacrament will help bring this about. In no other sacramental celebration are the personalities of both minister and recipient so determinative as to how the celebration will progress or how much of its potential will be realized. And in no other sacrament are both minister and recipient *encouraged* to take the initiative in making this a personal encounter.

As in every sacrament, the priest-as-confessor is a minister in two ways. He is minister, first, *of* the Church. As such, he is a representative of Church authority. It is he who offers the requisite satisfaction and pronounces sacramental absolution. It is he who, through words, gestures, and signs, proclaims the presence and power of the Reconciling Christ who is head of the Church:

> In the ecclesial service of the ordained minister, it is Christ himself who is present to his Church as Head of his Body, Shepherd of his flock, high priest of the redemptive sacrifice, Teacher of Truth. This is what the Church means by saying that the priest, by virtue of the sacrament of Holy Orders, acts *in persona Christi Capitis.*[4]

The priest is also a minister *to* the Church. Whether the sacrament is celebrated quietly with one other on a Saturday afternoon or enthusiastically with many others at a communal celebration, the priest is ministering to the Church. He is ministering to individual Christians who approach the sacrament for many reasons and from a broad spectrum of spiritual, psychological, and material situations. To be a minister *of* and *to* the Church is a compelling challenge, one Pope John Paul II has described as being both the most demanding, and the most rewarding, of a priest's ministry:

[The sacrament of Reconciliation] is undoubtedly the most difficult and sensitive, the most exhausting and demanding ministry of the priest, but also one of the most beautiful and consoling....Before the consciences of the faithful, who open up to him with a mixture of fear and trust, the confessor is called to a lofty task which is one of service to penance and human reconciliation. It is a task of learning the weaknesses and falls of those faithful people, assessing their desire for renewal and their efforts to achieve it, discerning the action of the Holy Spirit in their hearts, imparting to them a forgiveness which God alone can grant, "celebrating" their reconciliation with the Father, portrayed in the parable of the Prodigal Son, reinstating these redeemed sinners in the ecclesial community with their brothers and sisters, and paternally admonishing these penitents with a firm, encouraging and friendly "Do not sin again."[5]

The *Catechism of the Catholic Church* also comments upon the difficult, demanding, and consoling task the priest has both as the servant of God's forgiveness and as a pastoral witness to, and teacher of, the truth:

The confessor is not the master of God's forgiveness, but its servant. The minister of this sacrament should unite himself to the intention and charity of Christ. He should have a proven knowledge of Christian behavior, experience of human affairs, respect and sensitivity toward the one who has fallen; he must love the truth, be faithful to the Magisterium of the Church, and lead the penitent with patience toward healing and full maturity. He must pray and do penance for his penitent, entrusting him to the Lord's mercy.[6]

Ours *is* a lofty task: for the faithful often do open their hearts to us, their ministers and their teachers, "with a mixture of fear and trust." Our task too has its own mixture of fear and trust, of anxiety and concern. Some priests refuse to ask any questions or offer any but the most general of comments. Others are reluctant to do even this unless they judge it necessary for sacramental validity. "Why make a difficult situation more difficult?" is a valid concern. "I'm a minister of God's pardon and peace, not an inquisitor or therapist" is another comment on the right track. And many priests humbly sense they lack the knowledge or skills to engage their people in a dialogue that will be truly sacramental.[7]

Whatever the reasons may be, a certain reluctance on the part of the confessor *is* advisable. We want to be helpful, but we do not want to hassle. We want to offer the advice we think is needed in a given situation, but we do not want to come across as inquisitors. And never, certainly, do we want to intrude unnecessarily into the private lives of penitents, or add to the embarrassment of what for them may be an already difficult or awkward situation.

Respect for the dignity and privacy of our parishioners is as commendable as it is required. An automatic rule of "no dialogue whatsoever," however, is as ill advised as the opposite insistence of "questions always asked, comments always offered." A good question, a thoughtful comment, can be a powerful instrument for this sacramental ministry. It can reassure penitents they have been heard. More importantly, when a question is asked because what the penitent is saying is not

13

clear, such a question may be one of those "door-openers" that allows the confessor to minister more competently to this particular individual.

A SECOND PRINCIPLE: The words of the penitent

An effective minister of the sacrament of reconciliation learns how to let penitents help him minister to them.

Developing and refining our skills in "hearing confessions well" is a continuing challenge and goal. While no one statement says it all, a cardinal principle I suggest is this: *let the penitents help us minister to them.* One way of doing this is allowing them the opportunity (again, without demanding it) to tell us what is on their mind *and* what is in their heart. A wise question or two on our part may both encourage and allow them to do just that, as well as assure them they are heard. An example may clarify what I mean.

> A wife and mother in her late twenties confesses that she "really lost her temper and was cruel a few times to my children." What does she mean by *cruel?* Each of us confessors can and will interpret this in our own way. Was she uncharitable? Did she insult someone or talk about them behind their back? By cruel, does she mean she slapped someone? Does she mean that she hit her children? And if that, what about this "hit"? Are we talking about the "parental love tap," a spanking—or are we talking about a matter far more serious?

Not to ask a proper question certainly guarantees her privacy. It also means we may have forfeited an opportunity to respond effectively to her concerns and fears.

On the other hand, a question asked directly, gently— something along the lines of, "You mentioned you were cruel; can you give me a better idea of what you're talking about?"—also respects the woman's privacy and freedom. It remains her decision as to what, if anything, to say. But it also allows her *the opportunity to speak about her sin rather than simply confess it.*

Many times in our ordinary conversations, particularly when we are discussing matters of a personal or private nature, we want to say more but are reluctant to do so. We are uncertain how to proceed. Or we may fear what the reaction to our question may be. While the sacramental dialogue cannot be considered as just an ordinary conversation, often the same features and aspects of human behavior are operative. In the case mentioned above, we can give the woman a chance—a respectful, safe chance—to say more if indeed she may want to but needs some assistance or encouragement to do just that. A rule of thumb would be: *if it is not reasonably clear to us what a penitent is confessing, a respectful question or two may not only be appropriate, but may also encourage and help her to confess what she wants to confess—and, therefore, assist us in ministering to her.*

A THIRD PRINCIPLE: The words of Christ and his Church
The most important words we can say are the words of Christ and his Church: words of pardon, peace, and reconciliation.

That this book focuses on the nature, purpose, and potential of the *dialogue* in sacramental reconciliation is not to question the primary purpose of the sacrament. That purpose, of course, is to express and sacramentally effect the pardon and peace of God, the Father of Mercies. If nothing else is "accomplished" in the sacrament but this offering and effecting, then it is a good confession—and here I mean *good*

15

in a way that extends far beyond the canonical and sacramental requirements for validity.

This may seem obvious, but it does suggest another principle for our ministry in this sacrament, a principle that can be particularly helpful at those times when we feel overwhelmed, confused or, simply, "don't know what to say." The principle is this: *above all else, make sure that the reconciliation promised to every contrite, baptized Christian is expressed clearly and directly.*

There will be times when the specific, healing words we want to offer elude us or when, due to fatigue or perhaps our own heaviness of heart, we cannot find it within ourselves to express what we want and should. Without resorting to a minimalist theology that sees the priest merely as an impersonal administrator and the sacrament as simply an exercise of *ex opere operato*, let us remember the positive value of the Scholastic teaching. *Ex opere operato* does not refer to an automatic, perfunctory, cause-and-effect mechanism. Rather, it signals the humbling fact that forgiveness, while expressed through the Church and, it is hoped, expressed tangibly and visibly through the minister of the Church, comes from God. The power of love which is stronger than any sin comes from God and its effectiveness is assured by God. If we do nothing else but communicate that forgiveness clearly—and sometimes this may be done simply by praying the formula of absolution in such a way that it is clear to penitents that we believe what we are saying—they will not walk away confounded in their expectations.

One of the traditional values of the Catholic sacramental system is that God's offering of his grace is often mediated through others—in this case, through the sacramental ministry of the priest. I suggest that the effectiveness of the priest's *pastoral* expression of that ministry will promote the *sacramental* expression of God's offer of grace: a pardon and peace which is not simply pronounced upon penitents but which truly resides within them. Indeed, Pope John Paul II considers the interaction between penitent and confessor as one of the guarantees that the sacrament will speak sensibly and practically to the life of the penitent:

> The first form [reconciliation of individual penitents] makes possible a highlighting of the more personal—and essential—aspects that are included in the penitential process. *The dialogue between penitent and confessor, the sum of the elements used* (the biblical texts, the choice of the forms of "satisfaction," etc.) *make the sacramental celebration correspond more closely to the concrete situation of the penitent. The value of these elements is perceived when one considers the different reasons that bring a Christian to sacramental Penance*: a need for personal reconciliation and readmission to friendship with God by regaining the grace lost by sin; a need to check one's spiritual progress and sometimes a need for a more accurate discernment of one's vocation; on many other occasions a need and a desire to escape from a state of spiritual apathy and religious crisis.[8]

This correspondence to the concrete situation of the penitent is a fundamental value of the reconciliation expressed and effected through the sacrament. *This* person is offered God's pardon and peace—not in a general way, abstractly or theoretically, but for *these* particular sins. God does not deal with humankind abstractly, as the Incarnation proved. The *specific* response of God's forgiveness to the *specific* situation of a *specific* penitent is expressed most clearly by the confessor's *specific* response:

> In the Sacrament of Penance, the penitent has a personal encounter with Christ "through the ministry of the Church."

The priest as representative of the Church is also the representative of Christ, who is present in this moment to make objectively effective for each penitent as an individual the redemptive grace of the Paschal Mystery, which reconciles and heals.[9]

To the extent we understand and respond directly to our penitents—without forcing our way uninvited into their lives—to that extent will God's pardon and peace be expressed visibly and tangibly.

A FOURTH PRINCIPLE:
The words of the priest

The most important thing to remember in initiating or sustaining the sacramental dialogue is to remember why we are talking in the first place—and, especially, why we ask questions.

Just as we should not feel as though we *must* ask questions, we should never forget our motivation for asking them when we see the need. Father Karl Rahner warns against asking questions for improper reasons:

> [The purpose of questioning is] not to discover a *guilt* of which the penitent is not aware or which he is suspected to be keeping quiet....[We do not] ask as precise questions as possible in order to be able to evaluate the *guilt* of the penitent. For it must not be forgotten that the confession of the penitent is not an object for examination.[10]

The guiding principle in asking questions in the context of the sacrament—indeed, the only justification of any question—should be: *What (more) do we need to know that would help us minister to this person?*

In considering whether to ask a question, we must distinguish between what we *need* to know to minister effectively to this person and what we have a *right* to know. Recall the example given above, the woman who confessed she was cruel to her children. If we want to engage the woman and respond directly (and perhaps more helpfully) to her, we probably need to know something more about what she means by "being cruel."

A more complicated and delicate example is that of a fifty-year-old man who enters the confessional. Kneeling behind the screen, he confesses several sins including "a sin of impurity." As confessed, this "sin of impurity" could refer to masturbation, adultery, fornication, homosexual behavior, pedophilia, impure thoughts or desires, pornography...

We may think we know what the gentleman means and choose to leave it at that. We may remember that the canonical requirements for an integral confession[11] demand we need to know more precisely what it is he is confessing. Or we may wish to know something more about what this penitent is confessing so that we can minister more directly, more personally, to him. If we need or want to know more, it is there that the conflict or tension arises. We do not want to pry. We do not want to embarrass. We do, however, want to minister to *this* man. And we want to minister to him not in an abstract or theoretical way, but according to what he has brought to the sacrament. So *what*, exactly, is he confessing? What do we *need* to know in order to be able to minister more effectively to him?

If we elect to do more than "hear his confession"—that is, if we want to try to hear *him*—we need to know something more about what he is confessing. A carefully worded and calmly asked question will allow us just that:

You said you committed a sin of impurity. I thank you for your honesty on that. To help me, can you be a little more specific of

19

what it is you're talking about? Can you tell me what kind of sin of impurity you're talking about?

Again, our intention in asking such a question is not to make a difficult situation more difficult. What we are trying to do, figuratively, is slowly and respectfully "knock on a door or two" to see if he wants us—if he will allow us—to "enter that room." Our interest in that is not to be the voyeur, but to be a counselor, an advisor: one who reads the heart as much as that heart is opened to us. We pay a little more attention to the sin that is confessed so that we can attend more to the person confessing.

Admittedly, this is a difficult thing to do, for it is a delicate area in which we tread. We return to our example:

You said you committed a sin of impurity. Thank you for your honesty on that....Can you tell me what kind of sin of impurity you're talking about?

If the gentleman responds, "I had sex with someone," we have found something out. But is it enough to minister *to him, in his situation?* We may wish to know—for his benefit— if this sexual encounter was an isolated event, or if it is a pattern in his life. And we may wish to know—again, *so that we may minister to him rather than merely "hear his sin"*— whether his sexual behavior violates the faithfulness and integrity demanded by other relationships in his life. Once these questions are answered, we will be in a better position to respond more appropriately and directly to our penitent than were we to try to respond to "*a* sin against impurity." Here, though, we must again take care not to overstep our *right* to know. Further questioning about specific details, actions, locations, or situations may have a legitimate place in psychotherapy or long-term spiritual direction, but they are likely out of place in sacramental confession and are, therefore, an invasion of the penitent's privacy.

Again, the guiding principle concerning questions is this: *we ask questions to find out what we need to know that will help us help the penitent.* Asking the right questions—and only the right questions—will assist us in responding to the actual life situation of this penitent.

I realize that some priests insist we should never ask questions about what the penitent tells us. "God knows the whole truth, I don't need to," is the retort of one priest friend. Yes, God does know the whole truth. But God speaks through the sacraments of our Church—and God speaks through the Church's ministers of those sacraments. A key point underlying *sacramental* reconciliation (and all sacramental theology) is that a Christian does not have a relationship with God that is private, a relationship that excludes the community to which the Christian belongs. In celebrating the sacrament of reconciliation, Catholics encounter Christ *as they encounter him and the Church in the person of the minister.* God does know the whole truth. Hopefully, the words of the minister will allow that truth to be spoken—and heard—clearly, tangibly, concretely.

Asking appropriate questions is one way of honoring and respecting—and encouraging—the seriousness with which we wish all would approach the sacrament. I remember discussing my ideas about this book with six women, all of whom were in their early twenties. "What's the most important thing priests should remember when they're hearing your confession?" I asked. Their immediate comment didn't surprise me. "Tell them it's not easy for us to tell our sins," they all agreed. I then asked, "Does that mean you hope the priest doesn't make any comments or ask any questions?" "No, it's not that," they responded. One of the women clarified: "He shouldn't *keep* asking. But, you know, sometimes we wish he would ask a question or two. I mean, it's difficult for us to say what we want to say and, well, sometimes we need some help." One of her friends added a telling comment:

> What's really disappointing is when you've mustered up the courage to go ahead and say something and you actually want to talk about it—at least a little—and the priest just lets it hang. When it's something I was afraid of, but really wanted to talk about, I don't leave the sacrament relieved. I leave feeling I've wasted my time. Wasn't he interested—really interested—in what I was saying? Did he think I was just doing this as a matter of routine?

Father Karl Rahner expresses the same sentiment from the priest's perspective:

> If we [do not] carry out Confession with all our strength and in a more personal, more serious and more interior fashion,...if we act merely as machines for giving absolution, if we do not take man seriously and do not allow him to have his say, if we do not force him to take himself and God seriously or help him to find himself and to identify himself in a personal way, then these people will find that they are taken more seriously by the psychotherapist and they will go to him.[12]

I am not interested in turning the sacrament into a lengthy session of spiritual direction, pastoral counseling, or psychotherapy. The primary, fundamental focus of the sacrament of reconciliation is the sacramental effecting and showing of God's word of pardon and peace, not an ecclesial support group or self-help session. We do well to remember, however, that confession is the only counseling many will seek or receive. For some, it will be their only personal, direct encounter with a minister of the Church. Our primary responsibility as minister of the sacrament of reconciliation is to be a steward—an ambassador, as Saint Paul says—of God's reconciliation. That is primary. There are many times, however, when we can offer—and when we can be—more:

> In the dialogue with the penitent, the priests appreciate the personal dimension of the sacrament, which is brought to expression. It provides the opportunity to discuss with penitents the nature of sin as an offense against God and to help them to discern the causes and effects of sin in their lives. Individual confession provides a powerful sign of personal forgiveness.[13]

The desire to discuss and assist is not confined to priests. The just-cited study document also summarizes open-ended responses by the laity on factors influencing the frequency of their reception of the sacrament. It is interesting that the study reports that "the most commonly listed difficulty deals with the availability of a suitable confessor." Of the three groups in this category, one group represented those who "feel that confessors have not always taken their search for moral and/or spiritual growth and insight seriously enough."[14] These words bear witness to that conversation I had with my six friends.

A FIFTH PRINCIPLE: God's grace, God's time, God's plan

What then is Apollos? What is Paul? Servants through whom you came to believe, as the Lord assigned to each. I planted, Apollos watered, but God gave the growth. So neither the one who plants nor the one who waters is anything, but only God who gives the growth. (1 Cor 3:5–7)

I heard my first confessions thirty years ago. I remember nothing of the specifics of those confessions—*my* first experiences with the sacrament as its minister—but I do remember my attitude. I was determined I was going to be the best confessor any penitent ever had! Nothing wrong with that desire, to be sure. The purpose of this book is, after all, to help us become the best confessors we can be. But while my *intention* was on target those many years ago, what was off track was the *approach* I took.

I confess to a repeated mistake I made in those early days of my priesthood: I was determined I was going to solve the penitent's problem right then and there. No matter that she had gone to confession before, had confessed these same sins before, and had received advice and counsel from priests far more experienced and competent than I. This time I was going to make a difference—*the* difference.

I'm sure I wasn't guilty of massive malpractice in those early confessions, but I was guilty of excessive expectations. My expectations of what I could do and what my penitent might be able to do were too high. If she confessed anger towards her husband, I would feel obliged to offer her a half-dozen suggestions that would surely improve their relationship. If the young man confessed looking at xxx-rated films, I would proceed with a discourse on the value of sexuality in a way that would rival our late Pope's *Theology of the Body* (in length, though certainly not in quality!). No matter what the sin, the issue, or the problem, I was determined I would find the definitive solution this time, once and for all. My goal: after *this* confession, this penitent would never sin again!

Probably the only real damage I caused back then was that I kept my penitents in the confessional too long. There is no set time for a confession, of course, but I am sure that more than once I added a few minutes—and a few degrees of intensity—that were neither needed nor welcomed.

One suggestion I will offer in chapter 3 ("Some Things to

Avoid," point no. 3) is that the confessor should "not get lost in what he is saying," and much of what I write there certainly applies here. But here I focus not on a particular technique, but upon a fundamental attitude of the confessor towards himself, towards the penitent, and towards the sacrament. It is implied in the passage from Paul's First Letter to the Corinthians that opens this section, and might otherwise be stated as this: it is God's grace that calls us, priest and penitent alike, to conversion. And it is not our task to micromanage the power, the operation, or the timing of that grace.

Although it can be and sometimes is, the sacrament of reconciliation is *not* ordinarily a dramatic turning point in a person's life. More often, it is one of the many steps a person takes in order to grow closer to God. The example of Paul's conversion on the road to Damascus is admirable but it is not typical. Spiritual growth usually takes place much as physical and intellectual growth do: slowly, with false starts and frequent returns but, ultimately, with hope in the God who is at the beginning and end of all we do and are. Confession is not only about the forgiveness of sins. It is about conversion of life. Confession involves more than our expression of regret for our past. It calls us to express our hope for the future.

I will discuss some of the practical implications of this fifth principle later, under the question of "Refusing/deferring absolution?" (chapter 4, point no. 7). Here, I simply want to emphasize, as I did in the first principle, that for both priest and penitent the sacrament is an encounter with Christ. Both approach the sacrament to accept the offer of God's grace as he gives it, and not to determine the final disposition or regulate the timing of that grace.

Traditional moral theology knows of the "law of growth" or, as the *Vademecum* comprising Appendix I of this book refers to it, the "law of gradualness." This "law" reminds us that we ordinarily grow not by leaping from floor to floor but by walking up steps—and those steps often take the form of a narrow, winding staircase. People need time to grow, just as the seed of God's word takes time to take root in a heart and produce a harvest. While we can *absolve* sins, we may not be able to *solve* many problems. In many confessions the only thing that might be "accomplished" is assuring that our penitents know the sacrament as an occasion of grace, peace, and hope—no small accomplishment there.

A confession is not a failure if a solution to a problem eludes confessor and penitent. A confession is not worthless if stunning insights are not offered (or understood!). But a confession can be significant and meaningful to the penitent even if it is simple, brief, and without much drama. Many times, probably more than we realize, our ministry is to plant seeds in the hope and with the trust that God will give the growth in his own time and according to his plan. God's grace can have an effect over time that we cannot schedule, manage, or force—or even imagine.

The five principles I have discussed emphasize the value of our role as ministers of the sacrament of reconciliation. These principles speak also to the potential we, as ministers, enjoy and can use for the benefit of our parishioners. The grace comes from God, not us, but we are ministers and instruments of that grace.

Our parishioners come to the sacrament seeking a variety of gifts: forgiveness, assurance, comfort, freedom from guilt, an offering of hope. In one way or another, they approach the sacrament seeking *Christ.* The Church teaches that in such a case, Christ is there and the person will be addressed by Christ. Christ stands at the door, much as the Prodigal Father stood, waiting for the return of his wayward son. We do not place Christ at the door. But our words, our hopes, can open that door and help our parishioners see Christ more clearly than they might have dared ask or imagine.

Earlier in this chapter I referred to one author's contention that the power of the sacrament of reconciliation is akin to "quiet dynamite." In the next three chapters, I suggest a number of techniques—I offer a number of considerations— that can help us unleash the power of this sacrament, and so allow God's pardon and peace to fill the hearts of our people.

CHAPTER TWO

SUGGESTIONS FOR PRACTICE:

some things to consider

Confessors, penitents, and the "matters" of sacramental reconciliation come in a myriad of shapes, sizes, and situations. There are few rules, then, that will apply to every penitent and confessor in every situation. Moreover, what is not needed (and what is likely impossible to devise) is a set of formulae that purports to cover every sacramental celebration every time.

There are guidelines, however, that can help us engage the penitent in a dialogue that is pastorally beneficial as well as sacramentally effective. These guidelines suggest some of the things we should take care to do, as well as warning us about those things we certainly should avoid. In this and the following chapters, I offer a number of these guidelines.

In introducing this first set of guidelines, I refer to my remarks in the introduction to this book. What I offer are suggestions, not rules: things to consider at certain times, not procedures to follow always. These guidelines are based upon my experience and reflection, and I offer them to stimulate further thought and discussion, not to put an end to them.

1. Answer the fundamental question: why is *this* penitent here?

When a penitent enters the confessional, he brings with him his religious upbringing and his previous experiences with the sacrament (and with his confessors). How he has understood and experienced sin and grace in his life; how he thinks of God; how he is accustomed to approaching the priest and the sacrament: these factors shape his confession, for better or worse.

Does the penitent think of God as judge—or as the Father of Mercies? Does she see her confessor as a "channel" directing her plea for forgiveness upward and then pulling down God's pardon from above? Or in her eyes are we ministers in the true sense of the word: representatives of the Church and instruments and symbols of the grace of God? Does her examination of conscience and subsequent confession resemble a lengthy lamentation of legal violations? Or is her preparation for and celebration of the sacrament a time of accountability for her: a time when, with the help of God's grace, she renews her responsibilities as Christian, wife, and mother?

Why is *this* person here? Different people approach the sacrament for different reasons. The man who approaches the confessional with "God the judge" peering over his shoulder may be preoccupied with avoiding the fires of hell. The woman who describes her life as tedious and uninspiring may feel that God is more distant than present—representing a quite different perspective for her, and suggesting a different way of proceeding for us. The examples are plenty, and sometimes the first words of a penitent will give us a good indication of "why *this* person is here" and what *this* confession is about. The parishioner who begins with the comment, "I just can't seem to get my life together," is in a far different place spiritually and psychologically than the one who begins by saying, "I think I've already confessed this, but I just want to make sure."

So, too, the gentleman of fifty-five and the young adult of twenty-five may confess what are, objectively, the same sins. But while the first may be preoccupied with the future price he will pay for his sin, the latter may be concerned more about his lack of response to God's grace (or vice versa, of course). *Why is this person here?* To the extent we are able to answer that question, we will understand better what this person needs to be freed from. We will be better able to *respond to him* as well as absolving him of his sins.

Of course, we may not always be able to answer this question. We should remember, however, that the answers include forgiveness, reassurance, peace, freedom, sympathy, consolation, companionship, a request for prayers for a loved one who is sick, a temporary respite from loneliness—and, for some, a "stay of execution."

Why is *this* person here? *What does this person need to be freed from?* How *we* answer this question will suggest how we can respond *sacramentally and pastorally* to this particular individual.

Unless and until we have evidence suggesting otherwise, we should presume the penitent is making a "good confession." We recall that God's grace has called them to this sacrament, that God's grace guides them now, and that God's grace goes with them after his forgiveness is pronounced. This presumption in favor of the penitent helps us avoid what Fr. Bernard Häring has called the "sin of suspicion" in a confessor. If a penitent seems to be having difficulty in confessing, the difficulty is due more often to their embarrassment, shame, or frustration than it is an attempt to pull the wool over clerical eyes. *We* may have heard a particular sin confessed a number of times in a number of ways and, after some experience in the confessional, we may even be able to sense when the admission of a particular sin is about to happen. But, with the exception of our brother priests, no penitent has the confessional experience we do. Rarely will she have discussed with her friends how she should confess her sins. Rarely will she have the confessions of others to compare with hers.

In line with this, it is important to realize that we priests differ in our expectations of and experiences with the sacrament of reconciliation as much as our parishioners do. Just as our parishioners are more comfortable with certain "styles" of priests, so are we more comfortable with certain "styles" of penitents. Each of us tends to embrace a particular theology and practice of reconciliation, a theology and practice that has been formed by our experience and education. These preferences will not handicap our penitents or us unless we allow them to dictate our response to the extent that it is *our* needs, and not those of the penitent, that are being met.

2. Establish the focus of your remarks

Priests generally are careful not to look upon the particular sins confessed as so many different actions isolated from one another, but as indications of the penitent's overall state in life. Our seminary training has encouraged us to consider a confession of sins as a revealing of actions and attitudes that, taken as a whole, gives some evidence of one's fundamental relationship to God, oneself, and others.

Not a few confessions, however, may resemble a rather substantial list of what are, objectively, rather unsubstantial sins, failings, and foibles. To respond effectively is often difficult, particularly if we want to offer something other than an innocuous "you're doing okay" or "you can do better." We want to respond effectively, and so we try to find the pattern. We want to establish a context and so "absolve the person, not just the sins." But often a lengthy list has little or no "pattern" to it and it can be difficult to discern to what, if any-thing, we might pay special attention.

During one of the practice confessions in my class I was playing the part of a middle-aged gentleman who was con-fessing behind the screen....

> Been a couple of months, Father. Nothing too bad. Lost my temper a few times. Told a few harmless lies. Skipped out of work once claiming I was sick. I guess I haven't really prayed much, except with the kids at meals. Haven't paid a whole lot of attention during Mass all the time, either. A little swearing, some gossip a few times. I guess I've had some impure thoughts, too. I guess that pretty much covers it.

The deacon "hearing my confession" did his best, and from one perspective he did it well. Blessed with a memory for detail, he went through my confession offering comments and insights on each of my sins. "A little patience can help a lot with temper....harmless lies sometimes harm us because there's a reason we don't tell the truth....claiming to be sick and not showing up for work probably let some people down...."

It was clear my "confessor" had listened carefully to what I said, and that he was trying to give me some spiritual daily bread to chew on. His comments did come across, objectively, as encouraging and advisory, not condemnatory or scolding. Again, there is no one right way to hear this particular confes-sion, and my deacon confessor said some fine things, made some right moves, and gave some helpful advice. I learned some things about sin and grace from his comments.

The problem for this particular penitent, however, was that his confessor was taking a lot of time. And spending a lot of time in the confessional was something to which this penitent was neither accustomed nor with which he was comfortable. Playing the role of our middle-aged gentleman (and after two

decades of hearing confessions, I wasn't playing from theory),
I found myself first becoming uncomfortable. Then slightly
annoyed. Finally, I became somewhat concerned that my
priest was "going to go through the whole thing and just
how long is this going to take, anyway?" (Twelve minutes,
reported one of his classmates.)

In the review after the "confession," several students
remarked that while the "confessor" certainly had some good
things to say, it would probably have been better had he not
said it *all*. The next question was the logical one: *Which sins,
then, should he have said something about? When you hear a
number of sins that really don't seem to be related, how do you
choose which sins you want to comment on?* (Again, we need not
comment on any. My belief, however, is that we want to be
more than "hearers, penancers, and absolvers.")

How to choose, indeed. Here, I offer a principle I discussed in the previous chapter: *I let the penitent help me minister to him.* Such help can be invited by asking a question....

- *Among the sins you've confessed, which do you think
  are the most serious?*
- *Which of the sins you confessed bothers you the most?
  Which one(s) would you most like to do something
  about?*
- *You've mentioned a number of things for which you're
  sorry. You're saying you want to avoid them in the
  future. Which seems the easiest for you to fall into?*
- *What special grace would you like to ask of God in this
  confession?*

I have found these questions productive. And I have often
been surprised by what some penitents have chosen as "their
worst" or "their most workable" sins.

I believe I can offer a sensible or helpful comment on practically anything I hear. *How much better, I have learned, to invite the penitent to take the first step and give me some direction on what I might talk about.* I can do this by discovering which of my penitent's sins weighs on him the most. Asking the question, and then gently and appropriately pursuing the response offered, usually provides abundant "matter" with which to deal. More important, my question and his response will offer me a better perspective as to where this particular penitent is coming from.

Another way of responding to an "ordinary confession"—one in which numerous "daily sins" are confessed—is to offer our parishioners a different perspective on what is taking place in the sacrament. Instead of commenting on the sins they have confessed, we can talk about the sacrament they have approached. This approach is helpful when we see no need or have no desire to ask questions. It may be particularly appropriate when we are ministering to those who approach the sacrament frequently. Some possibilities for responding in these situations:

- *You celebrate this sacrament not only to confess your sins, but also to confess—to acknowledge—that you are sorry and want to do better. That's an important part of your confession, too. So, as you confess your sins, also confess—acknowledge—that God knows your confession and your heart....Confessing that—acknowledging that—is important, too.*

- *Once again you have come to confess your sins and ask for God's forgiveness. And so, again, let's be thankful that God listens to us. Let's be thankful that God is here, with us every day, every hour.*

34

- *What does your confession (this sacrament) mean to you? What is it you want to receive from this time of prayer and your confession?*

All three examples allow us to take an approach other than commenting on specific sins. And the last example is yet another of those questions that, if answered, may give us some guidance as to how to respond more directly to the situation our penitent feels herself in.

3. Use clear, simple language

Suggesting that we use simple, direct language does not mean we resort to a theological baby talk that would be insulting and condescending. We should not pepper our language, however, with terminology that would baffle *us* if we had not spent years in priestly formation and education.

During one practice confession, my confessor asked me whether I experience God as transcendent or immanent. I am familiar with the terms: I use them occasionally in lectures (which are where they belong!). But "in the confessional" I had to stop a moment and think about what he meant. If it seems good to ask that question, a simple "Do you feel God is close to you?" (or, "How close do you feel to God?") is likely a better way to proceed. On another occasion my confessor asked me, in view of what I had confessed, whether my fundamental option had been strengthened or weakened. "Are you living your life the way you think you should? Are you living the way you really want to? What do you think of your life?" These are questions that would be more understandable—even to the thirty-five-year-old PhD and mother of two I was role-playing.

I am suggesting we use language that is simple and direct, and I don't want this point to get lost in a flood of words. Curtly put: If we want to speak of conversion and repentance, then let us take advantage of all we know about that rich concept of *metánoia*. But let us do that in a language that will not be Greek to a penitent.

4. Give a penance that will "work"

Simplicity and directness are important also when assigning a penance—one aspect of confession many of us find difficult. First, some comments about the idea of "giving a penance."

When considering a penance, we should ask, *What do we expect the penance to do?* Or, better, what are we expecting our penitents to do with those prayers or good works? Do we understand the penance as a way our parishioners "make up" for the sins they have committed? Do we think of the penance as a challenge, a reminder, an aid, in turning away from sin and turning more towards God?

The introduction to the *Rite of Penance* states that "The act of penance [should] really be a remedy for sin and a help to renewal of life."[1] With this in mind, we want to offer a penance that is both effective for the person here and now as well as salutary for the world beyond. The theory is sound, but it seems easy at times to get lost in the ideals. A simple penance, expressed by simple words, has a better chance of fulfilling the ideal than a penance that is clever but complex.

Rather than sending our penitents to the pew to say a few prayers, many of us prefer sending them to the Bible. This is certainly appropriate, for the scriptures brim with stories of compassion, forgiveness, and the loving power of God. When we offer the scriptures as a penance, we should make sure the passage is familiar to our parishioners or can easily be found by them. "Read and think about the Parable of the Unmerciful Servant" may be the best possible penance in a given situation. But if we can't also immediately add, "It's in Matthew 18," we shouldn't expect our parishioner to be able to locate it either. Furthermore, the confessor who suggests spending some time with chapter 8, verses 10 to 15 or chapter 9, verses 6 to 15 of Second Corinthians is pointing to true gems of Saint Paul's wisdom. But will his parishioner know where to find them? Will she even remember all those numbers three minutes later—much less twenty minutes later when she returns to her home and her Bible? (Frankly, will she have access to a Bible?)

How, then, can we take advantage of the riches found in the scriptures? One priest resolved the problem quite imaginatively. He selected a dozen passages from the Bible, and then invested some time and money to have them printed individually on a conveniently sized, good stock paper. When he thinks it helpful, he gives—literally—his parishioners this scriptural penance. He likes the fact that he can give an appropriate penance for a specific confession. And he reports that many of his parishioners keep the scripture card for their future reference and prayer.

For "ordinary" confessions, an ordinary penance will suffice. The *Rite* indicates that the penance "may suitably take the form of prayer, self-denial, and especially service of one's neighbor and works of mercy."[2] Whichever form of penance we consider, we must offer the penance in a way that is understandable. Our parishioners usually do not go to confession the way many of us were or are accustomed to confessing in the seminary! "Just go out and spend a few minutes thinking about what God has done for you in this sacrament" is a penance that will be quite understandable to a third-year theologian. Offered in a parish confessional, however, we are likely to be asked, "Exactly what is it you want me to think about, Father?" or "How long did you say I should think about that, Father?" When this happens, it's clear that our parishioners—and we—are missing the point.

To assign a "creative penance" may be appealing and especially challenging, but a penance does not need to be creative in order to offer some help to our parishioners as they go about the business of trying to live as Christians. Depending upon their individual temperaments or situations, the best approach may often be simply to assign a standard or traditional penance in a creative way. This may include giving some specific suggestions about the penance:

- *Pray the Our Father once. But pray it slowly. Try really to pay attention to the words.*
- *Tell your wife that you are sorry. (Tell your wife that although you don't always say it, you do love her.) Is there something you can take home to give her that will help you do that?*
- *Put your Bible (prayer book) next to your coffeepot, and for the next week read (pray) from it for a few minutes while you're having that first cup.*
- *Promise yourself you'll say something positive about her the next time the gossip starts. And spend a few minutes today thinking of two or three of those positive things you might say.*
- *Say an Our Father now for this person. And then promise yourself you'll go a little out of your way to be nice to him in the office this coming week. It doesn't have to be anything dramatic. Just try to be nicer to him than he is to you.*
- *Come to church fifteen minutes early this Sunday. And spend that time looking at the gospel in the worship aid. Ask yourself what you'd want your son to learn from that gospel.*
- *Do you have a favorite prayer (scripture passage)? Say that prayer as your penance. Say it as a prayer of*

> *thanksgiving to God for his forgiveness, and say it as*
> *your asking for God's continued help in the future.*

People will admit that they have done hurt and harm and, occasionally, real damage. The stealing of another's money through theft, or the stealing of another's reputation through gossip and slander or of another's peace of mind through envy or lack of charity are sins that need to be confessed and that need restitution: restitution not designed simply for the eternal life we hope to enjoy in the future, but restitution for real life, in real time, here and now. Absolution is the pronouncement of God's forgiveness for the sins confessed but, as we know, forgiveness of the sins does not always undo the damage caused by those sins. As the *Catechism* notes, "One must do what is possible in order to repair the harm (e.g., return stolen goods, restore the reputation of someone slandered, pay compensation for injuries). Simple justice requires as much."[3] The seriousness of the offense—in some cases, the crime—need not take away from the respectfulness of our approach.

- *You've admitted that you've really done some damage to this person's reputation, and you're sorry about that. You've taken the first step. But that damage is still out there. What do you think you need to do to help this person out? What can you do?*
- *It's clear that you feel bad about the way you treated her. This is one of those bad feelings that's a good thing to have, actually. That feeling lets us know we've hurt someone else, someone who didn't deserve to be hurt. Let's talk a moment about that. What can you do for her that's going to help her? What can you do that's going to help both of you?*
- *You've confessed stealing a large amount of money. As*

> *you yourself have said, this is a serious sin. You've*
> *taken the right first step, but this is one of those times*
> *when it's important to think about how you can make*
> *up for the loss you've caused another.*

At times we might consider asking our parishioners what *they* think an appropriate penance would be. This can be particularly effective with those individuals who celebrate the sacrament regularly, and who obviously give some thought to their relationships with God, family, and friends (and enemies!). When ministering to those who have a habit of coming to confession, it is possible to encourage them to develop the habit of asking themselves what they need to do to strengthen their relationship with God and neighbor, and thus carry the power of the sacrament outside of the celebration itself.

There are times—when ministering to an especially scrupulous person, for example—when the last thing we should do is offer anything but a "standard, traditional" penance. I will discuss this further in chapter four ("Special Situations, Special People," point no. 2). And in the following chapter ("Some Things to Avoid," point no. 5), I give an example of a penance that, while well-intentioned, was counterproductive. To conclude this section, I offer five characteristics of a "good penance."

First, the penance should be *possible* and *reasonable*. This does not mean that a penance cannot be challenging, only that it be realistic—able to be realized. A penance that is unlikely to be said or done is not a good penance. "I'd like you to spend five hours doing some kind of community work or service for the church" might be an excellent penance in theory. But does our parishioner in fact have that kind of opportunity or time available? When offering a penance that involves some kind of action, we should ask if the penance we are assigning is, in fact, possible.

Second, the penance should *not be punitive.* This doesn't mean that a penance cannot be substantial. We should remember, however, that going to confession itself is seldom an easy task for most people. There are sins for which "work needs to be done"—serious breaches of charity, justice, and professional or personal responsibilities being at the top of the list. But let us consider the penance more as a way of helping a penitent make a better future, and less as a way of undoing the past—and certainly not as a way of purchasing or earning forgiveness. As John Paul II wrote, "Certainly [the penance] is not a price that one pays for the sin absolved and for the forgiveness obtained: no human price can match what is obtained, which is the fruit of Christ's Precious Blood."[4]

Third, the penance should *be sensible to the penitent.* It should make sense in light of what has been confessed. At times, then, we might offer along with the penance a brief explanation of why we are assigning this penance. For example, if a parishioner has confessed to us that he has spent well over a hundred dollars on pornography, we might ask him if he would be able to contribute a similar amount to a children's hospital or a charity, adding that "*I want you to have the chance to see the good your money can do.*"

Fourth, and related to the above point, the penance should be *associated with the sins confessed.* As the *Rite of Penance* notes, "[The penance] should serve not only as atonement for past sins but also as an aid to a new life and an antidote for weakness.…[It] should correspond to the seriousness and nature of their sins."[5] We might ask a woman confessing her lack of charity to a neighbor to speak some words of honest praise about that neighbor to others. Perhaps we can suggest to a student who confesses cheating that he spend an hour tutoring a classmate in need of extra help. We can counsel a man confessing envy or jealousy to consider sharing with someone less fortunate a resource he does enjoy.

Finally, the penance should have *clear limits*. That is, it should be able to be "accomplished" within a certain period of time. Penances such as "Say this prayer each day until you are no longer impatient" or "Do an act of kindness each day until you are no longer selfish" are bound to be frustrating and self-defeating.

5. Consider asking the penitent "*why?*"

"Why"—asking a penitent what led him to commit a particular sin—is one question many of us do not like to ask. We fear that to do so is prying into our penitent's life. Or we think that "asking why" could come across as judgmental or condescending. There are times, however, when "asking why" can be a way of helping our penitents help us minister to them.

Asking *why* about something a penitent has told us certainly is not done in a way that seems to say, "Well, now, what did you do *that* for?!" Our *attitude* in asking must reflect our *reason* for asking. And our reason, primarily, is to encourage our penitent to think for himself—to think *about* himself—in the context of what he has confessed. The following examples illustrate what I mean.

- "Father, I talk about my next door neighbor too much. She's the only one I have this problem with. I don't talk about other people."

  Why her, and not others? (It's good that you're not talking about others!) But what it is about her— about you and her—that is difficult for you to keep quiet about?

42

- "I tell a lot of lies, especially at school to my friends."

  When you tell lies to your friends, what's in it for you? Why is telling a lie to your friends easier—better—than telling the truth?

Sometimes asking about motives—asking the *why* about a certain sin—can yield unexpected answers, answers that encourage *us* to say something more. A confession similar to the following will be familiar to many of us:

Father, I guess it's been since last Christmas that I went to confession. Really not a lot of serious stuff to say. I lost my temper a whole bunch of times. Haven't always been nice in talking about others. I get jealous sometimes and act out of spite. Father, the worst thing is, I did miss Sunday Mass once, and of course I'm sorry for that. I think that's about it. Mainly the same old stuff.

We assume the confession is genuine. We may think it "unremarkable." It's a confession I always find most interesting to practice with my students.

Most of the student "confessors" deal with this penitent—she's a woman in her thirties—kindly and sensitively. Often one or the other offers advice about "temper" or "speech." And many times we hear some fine words about why it is fine—and why it can be important—to confess "the same old stuff" again.

After practicing this confession with several groups of students, I realized that none of the "confessors" questioned or commented on the woman's admission that she missed the Sunday Eucharist. In the standard review following the practice confession, I asked why. "I knew exactly what she was confessing, I didn't need to know anything else." "She only missed one time. This isn't a habit." "She knows it's wrong, she's not going to do it again." "She confessed it. I didn't want to call attention to it and embarrass her." "She was honest and direct about it. Why ask any questions or say anything about it?"

Understandable and reasonable explanations. And quite possibly many times in this situation, not asking the reason may be the better way of proceeding. Had one of the "confessors" asked *why*, however, he would have heard the following:

> Well, Father, my husband and I had been up most of the night. Actually the whole family was. Our little one was sick and was keeping us pretty busy. She was better the next morning, but my husband and I thought it better that I stay home and look after her while he packed up the other kids and took them to church.

We now have a quite different understanding of our penitent's "sin"! Clearly, it is no sin at all. We can and should point this out. And because we now know why this wife and mother missed Sunday Eucharist, there are other comments—comments helpful to her—we might consider making:

- *As I've said, your missing Mass under those circumstances wasn't a sin. In fact, I'd like to commend you on being a good mother.*
- *In addition to missing Mass, it sounds as though you really did "miss" Mass.*
- *Let me just ask how your other children felt about you not going to Mass with them. Did you or your husband talk with them about that?*

Asking why in this situation—and the subsequent dialogue between priest and penitent—can present a further opportunity to minister to our parishioner. We can reassure her she has not committed a sin. We can offer a little education about why this is so. We can suggest that she and her husband might be able to offer their children some education in Christian and family responsibilities and duties. These possibilities are additional ways we can minister to this woman, ways that go beyond sacramental absolution. But they are possibilities that would not have presented themselves if we did not ask that question, *why?*

Sometimes asking why a sin has been committed can help us answer that key question, "Why is *this* penitent here *now?*" For example, a gentleman enters the confessional and kneels behind the screen. From the sound of his voice, we judge him to be an older adult, perhaps in his sixties, maybe a bit older. After telling us his last confession was a month ago, he admits to missing some morning and evening prayers, being impatient, giving in to a few occasions of anger, and then confesses "the sin of self-abuse, about seven times."

The man's confession is straightforward, and there is no reason why we *must* ask him any questions. However,

> *You've made a good confession. I would like to ask you a question. Is there any particular reason why you are struggling with the sin of self-abuse?*

"Well, I guess, so, Father. My wife died not too long ago. We had a really happy marriage. These past couple of months have been pretty rough. I just feel a bit lonely and lost. I miss her."

Several insights might be gleaned by reflecting upon this brief illustration. First, some young confessors might be surprised that masturbation is neither a practice nor a concern only for adolescents and young adults and that, as may well be the case here, it often reflects an emotional loss rather than a sexual drive. Second, if we might be inclined to minimize his culpability in this regard, let us at least realize that it is a serious enough concern to our penitent that he mentioned it. Third, note the way "the why" was asked. By using the phrase "why you are struggling," we are implicitly acknowledging his contrition and his desire to do better. Fourth, the penitent's answer to our question tells us something very important about *him*, not just about specific actions here and there. We now are not only in a much better position to address him more effectively, but we also may see more of a need to take some extra time with him than if we had never asked our question. Finally, what we have learned may suggest an appropriate penance we can offer him:

> *I will say a prayer for you and for your wife. And in fact, I would like you to say a prayer for her as well. That will be your penance. Please say a decade of the rosary, with the intention of thanking God for the many happy years you and your wife had together.*

6. Know the occasion and take advantage of it

The occasion of a confession may be significant, and this may itself suggest an approach we might take. For example, first confessions of children are often times when the *parents* approach the sacrament after a long absence. Many times they are trying to set a good example by confessing on this particular night. Or, perhaps they have been encouraged (or humored!) by the mixed excitement and hesitation with which their children go to the priest. By acknowledging the good example the parents are setting, we encourage them to continue that good example. By acknowledging their response to the grace of the moment, we may encourage their further response to that grace. We need to remember that when we prepare or instruct children in any aspect of our faith, we are likely (re)educating their parents as well.[6]

Other occasions meriting special attention are the penance services celebrated during Advent and Lent. For many Catholics, these are the one or two times a year they approach the sacrament. And there are the "confessional nights" held in conjunction with the beginning or ending of a school year or religious education or confirmation classes. As for these "confessional nights," I offer a special comment, along with a heartfelt plea.

A religious education or confirmation class preparing for a penance service is an ideal opportunity for providing instruction concerning the sacrament to young, impressionable Catholics. Unfortunately, many priests will complain after such an evening, "They just don't know how to go to confession." This need not happen. We can work with our catechists and teachers and prepare these children and young adults for the sacrament. It would be well worth our while. More precisely, *it would be well worth theirs.* This is the ideal time to explain the sacrament and to speak of sin, grace, and reconciliation. It is the ideal time *to provide basic instruction on how to go to confession.* We need not return to the days when classes of students were brought to the confessional to admit the same sins in much the same words. My experience more than once with these special classes, however, is that many of our children, adolescents, and young adults not only have no idea of "how to begin" but—it becomes clear immediately—they have no real understanding of why they are there. (I will discuss this situation further in chapter four.)

Providing proper instruction in the *hows* and *whys* of the sacrament helps the next generation of Catholics approach the sacrament. Taking advantage of these opportunities for instruction is one way of fostering an appreciation for the sacrament and its practice in the years ahead.

There are times when knowing what is happening in the community at large will be helpful in helping us minister to them. I once assisted with a penance service for a large Catholic high school. In the course of some idle conversation before the service began, I learned that one of the school's most popular students and athletes had committed suicide only the week before.

Later one of the students was sitting across from me. He was "going through the motions" calmly, if not a bit disinterestedly, and it seemed clear to me he was "somewhere else." Acting on a hunch (Christians call it *grace*) I observed, "You seem preoccupied." For the first time he looked directly at me and, with a half-shrug, said, "Just got a lot on my mind." I waited a moment and then offered, "Like death?"

I will say no more about what occurred during our time together. I can say that what happened was as good as it was necessary. And I can say that what was necessary might not have been able to take place anywhere or anytime else. Again, while the sacrament ordinarily is not the time nor place for counseling or spiritual direction, for some it will be the only opportunity they have—or take—for such.

Know the occasion. Know what is going on in the community. Knowing these things can help make that dialogue between priest and penitent truly sacramental, truly a time in which the strength and love of God can be touched.

7. Memorize the formula for sacramental absolution

All priests should know the formula for sacramental absolution by heart. This suggestion is so obvious that I hesitate to include it in this list of "things to do." People will ask us to hear their confessions at unexpected times and in unexpected places. And that small plastic card will be nowhere to be found!

But there is a more pointed reason underlying my suggestion here. The words of absolution are at the heart of the celebration of sacramental reconciliation. Notwithstanding the words we offer our parishioners, these are the words "they wait to hear." These words, therefore, should come from our heart because we have taken them to heart. The more these words are part of us, the more we will speak them calmly, confidently, prayerfully. (And, when possible, while looking directly at the penitent. This certainly is better than the "tennis match" approach—turning our head from person to prayer card and back again.)

I remember one occasion when a brother priest hearing my confession concluded the sacrament by stumbling badly through the words of absolution. Having taken the formula to heart many years previously, I found it difficult not to be distracted as my confessor repeated himself, fought to find the right words and, in one instance, contradicted himself. To say that the confession was canonically valid and sacramentally effective is to miss the point. What is the point is that at the very time I would have liked to pay attention to the prayerful proclamation of God's pardon and peace, my confessor-induced preoccupation was "whether this guy was going to get through it or not."

Committing the formula to heart is helpful because we won't always have the ritual available. More important, it is one simple way we can take the time to take care that we have at least in some minimal way prepared for celebrating this sacrament ourselves.

Priests who enjoy some facility with languages might consider taking a few extra ministerial steps and learn the formula for absolution in a second (or third) language. Many of us have had occasion to spend time in non-English-speaking countries, and we know the relief and the joy of having a native of that country, whether in the restaurant or on the street, trying to address us in our language (no matter how imperfect the grammar or the pronunciation). A priest in any country who can at least absolve his "foreign" parishioners in their own language is certainly going beyond what is expected, and that extra distance he is willing to travel will be readily interpreted as an admirable gesture of care and respect for the penitent. We may not be able to learn a language well enough to comfortably hear a confession or confidently give sound advice. But here a little bit can go a long way, and pronouncing God's forgiveness in a person's own language is speaking the language of that person's heart. In most areas in the United States, Spanish is the second most important ministerial language; for convenience, the Spanish-language formula for absolution follows:

Dios, Padre misericordioso, que reconcilió al mundo consigo por la muerte y la resurrección de su Hijo, y envió al Espíritu Santo para el perdón de los pecados, te conceda, por el ministerio de la iglesia, el perdón y la paz. **Y yo te absuelvo de tus pecados, en el nombre del Padre, y del Hijo, y del Espíritu Santo.** (Amén.) ¡Que Dios te bendiga siempre!

8. Be hospitable

Obviously none of us sets out to be intentionally rude. But there are some very simple things we can do that will make a small, though positive, difference in the atmosphere. How we begin the celebration of the sacrament and how we end it are simple but important parts. Greeting the penitent with the words, *Peace be with you* (with hand extended when possible), already tells him something about how we see the sacrament.

Similarly, concluding with the prayerful dismissal, *Go in peace, God be with you*, again invites a response as well as closing the celebration on a peaceful note.

There are times when our hospitality is as simple as guiding the process of the confession. This seems to apply especially in face-to-face encounters. Unlike the preconciliar celebration of the sacrament, and the guidelines in the *Rite of Penance* notwithstanding, there is no "one way" for a confession to unfold. Some penitents begin right away; others wait for us to say the first word. Some parishioners may want to say a prayer or an act of contrition, while others expect their priest to begin with a short prayer or a brief reading from the scriptures. *How would you like to begin?* This question allows them to suggest the way the confession might proceed for, again, the answer may give us an indication as to why *this* penitent is here.

Another way of being hospitable is to give the penitent a chance to have her final word. I have often found it effective to ask, before assigning the penance, *Is there anything else you'd like to say?* My intent here is not so much to offer my penitents "one last chance" to remember a forgotten sin. It is to offer them the opportunity to respond to something we have discussed. And, sometimes, it allows them the chance to talk about something that is bothering them that is "not sinful." Again, we try to let them help us minister to them.

Finally, there are times when it is difficult to keep our eyes off the clock. A person will come to us for confession ten minutes before an important meeting we must chair. Or this confession follows immediately upon a complicated or painful encounter with another individual. We are preoccupied, feel hassled and, embarrassingly, we would like to "get this over" and give ourselves some breathing room or some time to think. At times like these, perhaps the best we can do is begin the confession with a few moments of silent prayer: a prayer asking God to guide the penitent, and a prayer asking that we remember that, all things considered, we were ordained for moments like these.

Obviously, penitents should never feel as though they are imposing upon our time. If there is limited time available, admit that at the outset.

> *I'm happy to hear your confession. Before we start, I want you to know that I have only about ten minutes. I'm sorry about that. Others will be waiting for me to be there. Is ten minutes enough time for you? Or is there another time that would be better?*

9. Know the Code—and the policies of your diocese

Celebration of the sacrament of reconciliation is governed by various canons, several of which pertain to complicated situations and procedures. Every confessor—new or experienced—should know the pertinent canons and, especially, his diocese's policies concerning the application of those canons. This applies especially to the remission of censures and penalties (e.g., the remission of the penalty for procuring an abortion), since policy details can vary from diocese to diocese. The following excerpt is from one diocese's document outlining the faculties enjoyed by its clergy:

> A priest may remit, either in the internal or external forum, a *latae sententiae* (automatically imposed) penalty established by law but not yet declared, so long as it is not one of the matters reserved to the Apostolic See. This faculty may be exercised only within this diocese's territory for any person actually in the territory regardless of where the penalty had been incurred. (Can. 1355) (NOTE: this is *one* diocese's policy; it is not to be understood as the policy applicable in every diocese.)

The offenses for which automatic excommunication is reserved to the Apostolic See are the following: desecration of the sacred species (can. 1367); physical violence against the pope (can. 1379); attempted absolution of one's accomplice in a sin of impurity (can. 1378); unauthorized Episcopal consecration (can. 1382); and a direct violation of the seal of confession (can. 1388). Therefore, a priest enjoying the faculties of the above-referenced diocese could remit the censure of excommunication (provided it has not been publicly declared) for the offenses of apostasy, heresy, or schism (can. 1364 §1) and—the situation diocesan priests will more likely face—procuring an abortion (can. 1398).

These canonical concerns can be confusing to penitents and priests alike. It is essential, therefore, that we know exactly what it is we are bound canonically to do and the pastoral concerns guiding our decisions. Furthermore, we should be able when necessary to explain to a penitent thoughtfully and to the point what a censure is and what procedures must be followed. These things we should know beforehand—before we find ourselves in the situation.

A thorough discussion of the canons and their implications is beyond the scope of this work. Resources readily available are the chancery, John Huels' *The Pastoral Companion*[7], and the *New Commentary on the Code of Canon Law*, commissioned by the Canon Law Society of America.[8]

10. Prepare to celebrate the sacrament— and "debrief" afterwards

We spend many hours each week preparing for our work and ministry. We draw up meeting plans and formulate budgets, draft schedules, and compose bulletins. We consider what we will say for the adult education class, the Bible study group, the weekly RCIA meeting, the baptism this Sunday afternoon. And of course we spend a good deal of time preparing our homilies. But do we prepare ourselves for our ministry as confessor? *How* do we prepare for that?

Sometimes, of course, preparation is not possible. The man who approaches us immediately before or after Mass; the woman who knocks on the office door: these people want us to hear their confession *now*. And so we do. Many other times, however, there is the opportunity—there is the time—to prepare for our ministry of peace. Parishioners do make appointments. Most parishes schedule a regular weekly time for confession.

Except for the newly ordained, none of us enters the confessional cold. Every time we begin to celebrate this sacrament we bring with us our knowledge, skills, and experience. I offer many suggestions and guidelines for hearing confessions in this book. But the best way of preparing to hear confessions is not to pull out one's notes and brush up on "techniques." Our best preparation for the sacrament is to set aside some time before we enter the confessional to reflect upon what it is we are about to do, and what it is we want to do. I refer to this two-fold preparation as, first, "entering the atmosphere" of the sacrament of reconciliation ourselves and, second, "fostering that atmosphere" for those to whom we will minister.

Entering the atmosphere. We enter the atmosphere of reconciliation best through our prayer. We pray that we may be sacraments of peace. We pray that we may see each person approaching the sacrament as a person of humility, a person of courage. We pray to remember that we say in this sacrament words no other person can say: we proclaim the good news of God's pardon and peace. We may recall the formula of absolution, reflect upon these words, and ask God that we may speak them confidently. Finally, we pray that we may listen with our heart as well as our ears; that we may speak with love as well as wisdom; and that when we speak, it will be the Spirit speaking in and through us.

Fostering the atmosphere. We do not know what will happen in this session's confessions. We do not know what we will hear, what we will say. In spite of all that we don't know, however, there is something we can do—something practical—to prepare for "today's confessions." As we continue to prepare to hear these confessions, we can see if the present liturgical season or the Sunday gospel speaks of reconciliation in any significant way. If so, that connection might suggest a general "theme" we might make use of in even the most "routine" of confessions. For example, we can point out to our penitents that the Sunday gospel is the Parable of the Prodigal Son (or that in the second reading St. Paul is telling us something about how to live). A brief comment on the passage, an encouragement to our penitent to pay special attention to the reading tomorrow: these are simple yet effective ways of "extending" the power of the sacrament.

After celebrating the sacrament, we would do well to spend a few minutes "debriefing." This debriefing obviously is not the kind that solicits comments on our performance, nor is it our detailed analysis dissecting what we have heard or how we have responded (although this kind of reflection on occasion can certainly be helpful). Having celebrated the sacrament, we debrief not by rehearsing the specifics of what has taken place, but by recalling again whose ministry we are offering. Having begun our ministry of reconciliation by spending some moments in quiet prayer, we conclude it that way as well. If our prayers prior to confession are those of calm and confident petition, perhaps our prayers after the celebration are characterized by thanksgiving: thanksgiving for the trust and confidence our people have placed in us, thanksgiving that through our ministry our parishioners have heard Christ's words of pardon and peace.

11. Honor the spirit, as well as the law, of the seal of the confessional

Two canons state clearly the Church's demands upon us regarding what we have heard in the confessional. Canon 983 §1 states that "The sacramental seal is inviolable; therefore it is absolutely forbidden for a confessor to betray in any way a penitent in words or in any manner and for any reason." Section 1 of Canon 984 holds that "A confessor is prohibited completely from using knowledge acquired from confession to the detriment of the penitent even when any danger of revelation is excluded."[9]

Although the canons are clear that the seal of the confessional is absolute, I have found that introducing the topic, whether in the seminary classroom or with laypeople, is sure to invite questions. Many of these are of the, "Yes, but what about the situation when…" type. The answer is always, simply, "If you learned about it in confession, then you don't know it." A classic example of this is as follows:

> [A] confessor knows that a certain person is a compulsive thief. The confessor is later appointed the pastor of a parish where that person is on the parish finance council. The pastor may not remove the person based on knowledge gained solely from the confession.[10]

It is important to understand that the pastor cannot remove "Mr. Smith" from his position on the finance council even if he were never to refer to Mr. Smith's confessions (either to Mr. Smith or to anyone else). As the canon states, a confessor cannot act on what he has learned in confession in any way that would be "to the detriment of the penitent even when any danger of revelation is excluded."

I have never met a priest who does not consider the seal of the confessional a most sacred trust and duty. Situations can arise, however, in which some might be concerned about, or at least question, the integrity of the sacrament even though we are in fact maintaining it absolutely. We may not be able to completely avoid these situations, but we can reduce the likelihood that our parishioners will have any reason to be concerned should they occur.

The first instance involves our preaching. Obviously our preaching is informed by our experiences, including the various aspects of our ministry. We learn a lot about human behavior through our ministry in the confessional, and we will no doubt share some of what we learn through our preaching. We should be extremely prudent in this regard, however. If we're preaching on a given Sunday about how harmful gossip and slander can be, it is likely that a few of our parishioners may wonder if we're using or thinking about their recent confession as our reference point. We won't be thinking of them at all, but of course that is exactly what we can't tell them from the pulpit! Whenever we preach on what might be considered "confessional matter," an extra dose of prudence and discretion in what we say and how we say it will assure that we keep what we must to ourselves.

A second occasion is that in which, shortly before we preside and preach at the Eucharist, we hear the confession of a parishioner who confesses some "matter" we are planning to address from the pulpit within a very few minutes! We have prepared our homily without their particular confession in mind, of course, but will they know that? In such an instance, it would be good—for them, for us, and for the notion of the seal—to offer a comment such as, "I want you to know that my homily this evening (or tomorrow morning) addresses some of the very things you've confessed. I just want to assure you that I'm not talking about you, and that I wasn't thinking of you while I was preparing my homily. But I do hope that what I say may be of some additional help to you."

There are times when parishioners will confess behind the screen and we will know who they are. Perhaps they are regular penitents, or maybe we recognize their voice or unique way of speaking. In these situations I believe we should respect their apparent desire for privacy and not address them by name. Many of us have had the experience of a penitent coming around the screen to shake hands or extend greetings after he has confessed "anonymously." But that self-identification is his decision and is taken at his initiative, and we should not presume to call a penitent by name—unless it is clear that they know or assume that we know who they are. (Besides, there is always the chance we'll get it wrong and that would be awkward indeed!)

When a parishioner confesses to us regularly, we may refer to what he has told us in previous confessions. That is one of the values of having a regular confessor: over time the priest gains a better understanding of this particular penitent's virtues and vices, and is in a better position to offer advice and counsel. But what we have learned can be referred to only during subsequent *confessions*, not on other occasions unless, again, the penitent takes the initiative. If Mr. Jones approaches us after Mass and asks us again the name of the book on gambling addictions we mentioned in his confession last week, we are free to tell him. Obviously his bringing the subject up "opens" up his confession for our responsible reference. Different, however, would be our approaching Mr. Jones with the comment, "Oh, I wasn't aware of this book last week but I just happened to come across it yesterday and, considering your confession, I thought it might be of some help to you." The rule: any initiative outside of the confessional regarding a previous confession must come from the penitent, not the priest.

Finally, the adage about actions speaking louder than words presents an ongoing challenge to me and to every confessor. As I mentioned above, I have never met a priest who does not hold the sacramental seal as a sacred trust and duty. But I think many of us would acknowledge that we may at times unwittingly discourage others from going to confession to us because of the uncharitable or angry comments we may make about others in everyday conversation. It's not that our parishioners think we would go out and disclose their sins to others. But a priest whose behavior and speech are marked by criticism of and scorn for others does not promote the peace and integrity we hope to offer through the sacrament. I discuss this further in Appendix III, "Confessors Need to Be Penitents, Too."

CHAPTER THREE

SUGGESTIONS FOR PRACTICE:

some things to avoid

In the previous chapter I offered eleven guidelines that can help us engage in a sacramental dialogue with our penitents, a dialogue that allows our penitents to experience God's forgiveness in a tangible, personal way. These guidelines—again, they are suggestions, not rules—belong to the general category, "Consider doing this."

In this chapter I discuss a variety of things we should take care *not* to do. None of my caveats concern things we deliberately set out to do: we do not enter the confessional with the express intention of accusing or insulting the penitent! But one reason why being a minister of sacramental reconciliation is often a demanding task is that, in this personal and sensitive atmosphere, always we must not only consider what we say, but pay special attention to how we say it.

Many of the admonitions and caveats I offer in this chapter are obvious. The path to their commission, however, is often as indirect as it is subtle.

1. Do not accuse; do not insult

None of us wants to change the sacrament of peace into a time of accusations. Yet, we can ask questions that, well intentioned though they may be, are thoughtlessly worded and so smack of an accusation:

"You say you got really upset with your wife a few times and lost your temper. Did you strike her?"

Certainly the tone of our voice and our prior relationship with this gentleman (if such exists) will influence how he will receive our question. Taking the question as it stands however, I point out a possible danger. If the husband did strike his wife, he may resent the rash, abrupt question. He may resent that we immediately assumed rather than listened patiently, and so have taken away his initiative in saying more. He may feel backed into a corner. Because the question has come at the beginning of his confession, it may not set the best mood we would hope to establish. On the other hand, if the gentleman did *not* strike her and his confession is his sincere effort to continue becoming the good husband he wants to be, it may require considerable compassion and understanding on *his* part not to be offended by our rash question and judgment.

If we feel the need to ask a question here, a better and more respectful way should be sought: *What happens to you when you lose your temper with your wife? What do you think? What do you do?* Questions such as these are more gentle and respectful. They tend to "open up" the possibilities for dialogue. Our gentleman probably will not only answer our question, he may well also tell us something important about the way his life is going.

None of us wants to accuse, and none of us wants to insult. There have probably been times in the confessional, however, when we wish we could take back something we said. We offered our words with the best of intentions. Or perhaps we just didn't think before we spoke. At any rate, what we said was interpreted in a way we did not, or could not, have envisioned. Consider the following questions: how they might come across to the penitent (in this case, a young adult man), and whether there may be a better way of asking them....

- *You [young man] confessed having impure actions with someone. Was this with a woman or with another man?*
- *The sin against sex…was this just a "one-night stand"?*
- *Do you have sex with this person often? Have you had sex with this person before?*

Let us presume we have asked these questions with good intentions. We did not ask them to satisfy our curiosity, but to help us respond better to our parishioner. We seek a better understanding of where our parishioner is in regard to sexuality, relationships, and his overall situation in life. We want to attend to the person, not just pay attention to his sin.

Because of the way we have asked these questions, however, our good intentions may be eclipsed by our poorly phrased queries. The first question, for example, raises the possibility of homosexual behavior. This may be the case, but asking that question at the beginning of our dialogue may come across to our penitent as intrusive. Moreover, if our penitent is not confessing *homosexual* behavior, he will be offended and insulted by our insinuation.

The second question assumes that the penitent's sexual behavior was an uncharacteristic lapse, and not a "habit." But the question is far from being complimentary. "Just a one-night stand" sounds flippant and disparaging. Are we suggesting that if it was a one-night stand it really doesn't amount to much? Or are we suggesting that our parishioner would want to involve himself with another person in this way? The third question tends to be blunt and accusatory from the opposite perspective.

If, in this instance, we think we need more information for the benefit of the penitent, i.e., *to help us minister to him,* a more appropriate way of seeking that information should be considered. The following questions, for example, "open doors." They allow the possibility that we will know what we need to know to minister to this person. They allow us that possibility while still leaving the penitent "in charge" of his or her admission....

- *Can you tell me what kind of relationship you have with the person?*
- *Sexuality is an important (sacred, holy) part of our lives. Can you tell me something about how important this person is to you?* (The necessary follow-up here, of course, is that if the sexual partner is someone important to the penitent, the importance of the relationship does not condone the sexual acting out.)
- *Can you say something about how the sex has influenced your relationship with this person?* (Again, the necessary follow-up, as above.)

These questions will give us the information we seek in a way that respects the young man and honors his privacy more than the first set of questions. And since questions asked in this way also suggest more clearly the confessor's reasons for asking (a desire and willingness to help, not to judge or satisfy one's curiosity), they allow the penitent considerable freedom as to whether—and how—to answer. Another example:

Penitent: I got drunk and ended up doing some stuff I didn't want to—and ordinarily wouldn't have. It was the alcohol more than it was me. But I kind of made a mess of some things and I'm really sorry about that."

A possible response: Well, if it was the alcohol don't worry too much about it. Those things happen from time to time. (This is an unfortunate response: it does not take the penitent seriously. What he did is important enough to him that for some reason he is bringing it to confession. If he isn't willing to dismiss it automatically, then neither should we.)

A second possible—and hasty—response: You say it was the alcohol. Are you an alcoholic? (An abrupt question: accusatory, insulting, presumptuous.)

A third possible—and more thoughtful—response: What bothers you the most? What you did, or that it seemed to be the alcohol doing it? (This question opens several doors, and without slamming any of them in his face. To the extent he answers this question he will be helping us help him.)

Do not insult, do not accuse. We do not intend to commit either of these offenses. By responding in a thoughtful way—in a way to which some thought has been given—we will minimize the chances that we might do so unintentionally.

2. Do not draw quick conclusions

Assumptions and presumptions are risky anytime, anywhere. In the sacrament, they can be most counterproductive. A particularly instructive example of how easy it is to quickly draw the wrong conclusion—and the counterproductivity of it—comes, fortunately, from one of the practice confessions in my classroom.

Confessing behind the screen as a "sounds like a man in his fifties or so," I admitted "sinning in action against the sixth commandment." My confessor had the best of intentions. He wanted to speak directly to what I had confessed, and so respond to what he assumed was my state in life (a husband and father). My confessor was compassionate. He did not want to ask for specifics, because he did not want to embarrass me. He did not want to put me on the spot. After all he knew the sin I was confessing. So he thought. So he assumed.

In this case, however, his compassion and good intentions led him astray. He delivered a brief and excellent commentary on how important marital fidelity is, and on the hurt and pain that breaking that bond can cause. He then said, calmly and compassionately, that my confessing breaking my marriage vows could be an opportunity to reconsider my relationship with my wife and, once again, pledge her my love and fidelity.

After the confession the class reviewed what had taken place. My confessor admitted he was puzzled that I had been so quiet during his words of encouragement. He thought, though, that I was probably embarrassed—or, perhaps, that what he was saying to me was really striking home. Clearly, he *was* trying hard to be a good confessor, a good minister, to me.

Finally one of his classmates asked whether adultery was really the sin I was confessing. I replied that it was not. We then discussed how, in a "real situation," this middle-aged, faithfully married husband might have reacted. He had confessed masturbation *the way he was accustomed to confessing it.* His confessor, having drawn another conclusion altogether, seemingly "went off on a tangent," even suggesting to him that he had cheated on his wife.

The point is clear. We do not pry. We never ask questions that are superfluous or unnecessary. *But if we are going to respond to what a penitent has confessed, we must know what it is he is confessing.*

3. Do not get lost in what you are saying

I offered one example of the hazards of saying too much in the preceding chapter (point no. 2). I return to the principle underlying that example. The sacrament is *ordinarily* not the time for a lengthy lesson in sacramental or moral theology. When it is necessary to offer some insight or instruction in these areas, our words should be to the point. Ordinarily, we do better when we set aside the finer points of theology and instead speak to what is happening now: the courage and honesty of confronting one's sin, and the response of God's forgiving love.

Do not say too much. I do not encourage the "quickie confession" here: I agree that the sacrament does provide us with opportunities for moral instruction and exhortation. I simply underscore again the importance (for us and for the penitent) of that fundamental question referred to above: *Why is this penitent here?*

Many penitents *are* interested in what we have to offer them by way of theological insight and moral guidance.[1] For others, the first and perhaps only priority, however, will be to *take care of their business with God*. We want to offer as much as we can, but we shouldn't forget that the primary purpose of the sacrament is expressed well in the words of absolution.

Seminarians understandably want to "get it right" and so many times in class I am asked, *How long should a confession last?* When I respond "as long as it needs to," I don't intend to be flippant. There is no standard time for a confession. What will determine length are considerations such as what is confessed, how often the penitent celebrates the sacrament, the style of confessing, *what brings the penitent to confession at this particular time*, the time available, the number of people waiting for confession, and the like. Recalling one parish weekend experience, I heard five confessions within fifteen minutes, and I do not believe any were rushed or hurried along, either by the penitent or me. The sixth confession took somewhat longer—not because it was the last confession of the afternoon, but because "it needed to take longer." Assuming and moving a bit beyond the concept of sacramental effectiveness, the *significance* of a confession to a penitent is measured neither by its brevity nor its length, but by the degree of divine, ecclesial, and personal forgiveness and reconciliation experienced by the penitent.

4. Do not neglect to say what must be said

"Do not say too much....do not say too little." These two guidelines are not as contradictory as might seem at first. The point of the preceding suggestion is that if there is no need for us to speak a lot, then we should not speak a lot. The point here is that *at times a response is not only appropriate but also desirable.* I offer one example here, and refer to another example I will discuss in the following chapter.

The "difficult" confession

When a parishioner has obviously struggled to make her confession—perhaps because of what she had to confess—we should acknowledge the very difficulty of the confession. In line with what we have previously discussed, we may or may not ask a question or offer a comment. But in the case of a "difficult confession," and before any questions are put forth, there is something we can say that can itself initiate a dialogue that can be truly sacramental.

What defines a difficult confession, of course, will vary from penitent to penitent. For the spouse it might be confessing marital infidelity; for the unmarried it might be sexual behavior with a friend—or with an acquaintance or even a stranger. And, let us not seduce ourselves by thinking that the land of the sixth and ninth commandments has a monopoly on "difficult-to-confess-sins." Women and men of all ages struggle to acknowledge and take responsibility for uncharitable, sometimes hostile, acts towards friends or family, as well as the sins of stealing, lying, slander, and gossip. For some people, acknowledging *any* sin—any fault—is embarrassing and difficult.

When a penitent confronts her pain and embarrassment and confesses a difficult sin, let her not do so in vain. We should assure her that we have heard both her confession *and* her difficulty in confessing. There are several ways we can offer this assurance.

We may acknowledge the "grace of the moment" that has brought her to her painful honesty. Later in the confession we can appeal to her courage as an example—*her example*—of the courage needed to continue turning away from sin:

- *It was difficult for you to say this, wasn't it? I respect your honesty and your courage.*
- *I sense that it was difficult for you to confess what you did. I'm glad you did; it says something about how serious you are about your life.*

Perhaps an even better response, one that invites the penitent to respond on her part, is the following:

You certainly have shown some courage in confessing that. Where does that courage come from? This was a hard thing to bring to confession. How were you able to decide to grit your teeth and go ahead and mention it?

Such statements speak volumes. They assure penitents that we are taking their confession *and their experience in confessing* seriously. Many of us are familiar with the time-honored and traditional response on the part of the confessor, "Thank

God for the grace of having made a good confession." It is unfortunate that some see this response only as a theological cliché to rely upon when "nothing else comes to mind." Properly understood, the "grace of a good confession" can only refer directly to the courage and honesty that assists one in making a good, grace-ful confession.

A second instance in which we should not "say too little" is when a penitent returns to the church (and the sacrament) after a long absence. I will discuss this in the following chapter (point no. 9).

5. Do not complicate or "extend" the confession for the penitent

We want to assign a penance that truly is "a remedy for sin and a help to renewal of life." At times our zeal in doing this may end up being counterproductive. As the following example suggests, a penance that might be helpful from the confessor's perspective can be for the penitent a somewhat torturous extension of an already difficult experience.

> He still remembers the experience because it terrified him. He was twelve years old, and his endocrine system was working overtime crock-potting that stew of hormones that pushes us into adolescence. It was the early 1960s, and the prevailing Catholic culture had him going to confession once a month. So, he entered the box one Saturday afternoon and shyly admitted to those sins characteristic of twelve-year-old boys. To no one's surprise but his, impure thoughts and sexual fantasies were at the top of his list—but among the last he confessed. Finally, thinking the worst was over, he relaxed a bit and prepared to receive his penance.

My friend still remembers the experience because it terrified him. "I want you to talk to your father about these impure thoughts and fantasies," his confessor told him. "And talk to him about it before you come to confession again."

Talk to his *father*? About dirty thoughts and desires? *About sex*? To his father? No way. Unlikely. Impossible. Forget it.

But he couldn't forget it. *It was his penance.* And he had been taught that he must do his penance for his confession to be "good." If he didn't, things would get worse. The next time he went to confession he'd have to start all over again and confess that too.

He says those next few weeks sped by. He dreaded that next confession: dreaded it because, once again, he would have to confess his "sins against sex." He dreaded it especially because he knew he wouldn't be making a good confession until he had performed his penance and talked with his father. My friend smiles about it today, admitting that he did talk with his father about it all—for about two minutes, in the car, as they were pulling into the church parking lot a month later. He chuckles that it seemed to be a penance as much for his father as it was for him. And he recalls, though he did not know this word so many years ago, that his penance was "counterproductive." The sacrament of peace had become an occasion of terror. The penance he had been given—frankly, of doubtful spiritual or psychological value—had become, not a means of conversion, but an obstacle.

Sacramental reconciliation is a means to conversion, a means by which we can continue to grow spiritually and psychologically. It is a way of *experiencing* God's pardon and peace. But my friend experienced little of that those many years ago. He experienced more embarrassment than he should have, more shame than he knew how to handle. Worst of all, the approach of his next confession became, not an opportunity for grace, but an occasion to fear, dread—and, if possible, to avoid.

The sacrament of reconciliation is celebrated ordinarily within a few moments' time. Our hope is that the peace it offers—and the challenge—will last in the person's life long after the celebration of the sacrament has concluded. Our words, our attitude, the penance we offer: these are ways we can help the sacrament "endure" in the lives of our parishioners. But our words should take account of the parishioner's state of life: his age, his probable ability to understand and, as in this case, the real likelihood of his being psychologically and emotionally capable of fulfilling his penance. Above all, we should make sure that our penance does not make things more difficult for our penitent—and that, as in the example above, it ends up being a painful and needless preoccupation for him, rather than promoting his desire and his ability to live the Christian life.

6. Do not "reconfigure" the penitent's confession—or the penitent's conscience

It is one thing to help our parishioners, when we are asked, with their examination of conscience. It is quite another to "take the ball of sin and run with it"—or, even worse, for a confessor to add layer upon layer to the penitent's confession, thus creating a "penitential snowball." With the explicit permission (and encouragement!) of several priest friends, I present the following situation—a composite of several experiences in spiritual direction and in the sacrament that were frustrating, demeaning, and unnecessary.

> The priest had wanted to celebrate the sacrament (as the one confessing) for some time. But embarrassment and shame (and, in no small part, the absence of a suitable, that is, "anonymous," confessor) kept him from the sacrament far longer than he would have liked. Realizing an opportunity

soon would be available, he set aside a half-day of prayer and reflection to prepare for the sacrament.

When the time came he sat down in front of a brother priest and began by describing his "state in life." He gave his age, the fact that he was a priest, and he spoke a bit about his ministry. Then he confessed his sins.

He talked not only about how he had come to sin, but also about his "firm purpose of amendment." In this, he spoke of specific and practical steps that would help him on his way. He described how he had let his shame and fear keep him away from a sacrament in which he had always found great peace and comfort. He concluded by repeating several resolutions he had already adopted to "amend his priestly and Christian life." This young priest-as-penitent was in no hurry. He had prepared carefully for this time. It was a time he hoped would be truly a celebration of his "return to grace," a time of thoughtful, reflective renewal of his baptismal and priestly commitments.

But the first words spoken by his confessor effectively ended his hopes—and his experience—of this being a celebration of reconciliation:

"How many Masses have you said since you've been in the state of mortal sin? You received communion at each of those Masses, didn't you? And what about the stipends? I assume you've been accepting stipends all along—all the while you were in mortal sin. Now let's go back through this whole thing, from the very beginning. There are a lot of things here you haven't confessed."

I do not dispute the point that, technically and canonically, the young priest should have included "Masses, communions, and stipends" as part of the "matter" of his confession. What is unfortunate is that these things seemed to be the primary focus of his confessor's approach. *If* the young priest-as-penitent should have included these points; and *if* his confessor thought that these points really needed to be mentioned; there are far better ways—better pastorally and sacramentally—the confessor could have chosen to bring them to the confession.

What is perhaps most unfortunate is that "extreme examples" such as this one will not seem unlikely to any priest who has listened to his parishioners talk about their experiences in the confessional. Perhaps the only fortunate aspect in this example is that the experience was inflicted upon a young priest who knew, from his own (and better) experience, that most confessors do not take an approach that is, at best, misguided or thoughtless. This young priest did not allow his confessor's ineptitude to keep him away from the sacrament again. Many parishioners, however, might not be as patient, understanding, or forgiving.

The lesson? Recall Father Karl Rahner's sage advice that we do not ask questions "to discover a *guilt* of which the penitent is not aware or which he is suspected to be keeping quiet….For it must not be forgotten that the confession of the penitent is not an object for examination."[2] If the young priest's confessor had been listening *to him* (and not just to "his sins"), he would have had no reason to be concerned about hidden sins or concealed faults. He would have felt confident this was a good confession because he would have seen his penitent as a "good confessee": a man who was contrite, reflective, conscientious (which does not mean figuring out every canonical angle), and determined to do better. Unfortunately, not one of these qualities merited a comment—or, perhaps, even was noticed.

7. Do not make the penitent's confession *your* confession

The appropriate sharing of our lives is to be encouraged. We bolster our growth and our competence as priests when we share our ideas and our hopes, our fears and our struggles, with our spiritual director, our brother priests, and with other close friends. These people help us grow emotionally and spiritually just as, hopefully, our support and understanding of them is conducive to their growth.

Sacramental reconciliation, however, is *not* the same as a mutually intimate conversation with a good and trusted friend. The confessional is a place of intimacy, to be sure; but it is a unique intimacy in that the *nature* of the encounter defines and determines the intimacy as much as the words that are spoken. Parishioners enter the confessional to confess *their* sins, not to hear ours. When a priest chooses to "share," i.e., to be *self-revelatory* in the confessional, it must be done with caution, tact, and prudence.

This is particularly true in the area of sexuality because *good intentions carelessly executed can lead to serious harm.* When a penitent speaks of difficulties in dealing with sexuality, we must consider carefully if and how we "put ourselves into the situation." Here I am not referring to those situations when the confessor's questions or comments might be misunderstood and suspected of being (or accepted as) solicitations. The potential for serious harm in these cases is obvious. Rather, I note here a danger much less dramatic and publicly damaging than "solicitation," but one which, because of its subtlety, can be overlooked.

Consider this nineteen-year-old male collegian who is taking advantage of a Newman Center Retreat to come to confession:

Penitent: Father, I'm hung up on sex. Put simply, I mastur-
bate a lot. A few days will go by when I don't, and then I'll
do it every day for a week. Sometimes even twice a day. I
know some people think it's no big deal, and I've read some
stuff that says it's just all part of growing up. But, I just don't
feel good about it.

Confessor: I know chastity is difficult at your age. Well, you
know, it's difficult to be chaste at any age, especially when
you're single. You aren't the only one who's bothered by
things like this. I struggle a lot with chastity too. It's not easy
for me, either.

We have a young college student who, not atypically, is
preoccupied with genital expression and pleasure. He confesses something he wants to confess or at least feels he needs
to confess. We do not know exactly how he views masturbation and his being "hung up on sex," but it is clear he is not
entirely at peace. He feels bad enough—or confused and
frightened enough—to acknowledge his problem in the context of the sacrament.

His confessor tries to be compassionate and understanding. He wants to help the student put things in perspective.
He wants to offer him some knowledge and insight from his
experience that the young man does not, and probably cannot have, at this point in his life. These, certainly, are worthy
intentions. They are the kinds of intentions that can contribute to making the dialogue sacramental.

But *what message might be understood* by his self-revelatory
comments? We know that people do not always hear what is
meant, and intentions behind a statement do not always coin-
cide with how the statement is interpreted. In this case, the
confessor means one thing but the penitent may understand
something quite different. While the penitent may greatly
appreciate the compassion and understanding with which he

is treated, he could become confused about whether he has a problem at all. He might interpret the confessor's understanding and compassion as, *Don't worry about it. Everybody has problems with chastity—even I do.* As the confessor tries to offer understanding and compassion, the priest may forget that, most definitely at this particular time, he offers himself as a minister of the Church: as one who represents certain values, ideals, and a way of life.

Similarly, the word *struggle*, especially concerning chastity and celibacy, carries among priests well-understood and acceptable connotations. But that same word may be interpreted differently by others. The compassion and understanding underlying the confessor's statement, *I struggle a lot with my own desires and fantasies as well,* may not be what impresses the young man. He may leave the encounter thinking that the priest has much the same problem with masturbation and sexual thoughts as he does—a message the confessor does not intend at all. Although the confessor's quite respectable intention is to reassure and support this young man, the priest's words might not only *not* do that but also might, in fact, further confuse and frustrate him.

I do not suggest that we portray ourselves—much less that we think of ourselves—as immune to all temptation or innocent of all sin. People need confessors who are compassionate, not perfect. But a compassionate confessor is not one who, in the context of the example, *seems to be having as much trouble with sex as they are.* If we need to reassure penitents that they are "not alone in all of this," we can offer that reassurance without specifying or inappropriately suggesting whatever particular struggles, confusions, and difficulties we may have. Many people approach the sacrament to lighten their spiritual and emotional burdens. We must not add to their burden by indiscriminate or careless sharing.

Finally, the clergy sexual abuse scandal impresses upon us the need to add an extra measure of prudence and care to our actions and words. Especially when discussing with a penitent matters or concerns of sexuality, the importance of maintaining professional boundaries and avoiding unnecessary questions cannot be overstated. A penitent's misinterpretation of our well-intentioned sharing of our experiences or struggles can lead to tragic consequences for us, our penitent, and the Church.

8. Do not make the penitent's confession your confession—a second version

One responsibility we have as confessor is to encourage a good confession—in the many ways "good" can be understood—*for the penitent*. We may think that a particular penitent *needs* to hear something from us. If so, let us offer it. But if it seems that she is *unable* to hear it, we should not force it upon her. As confessors, our role is not to assure that this particular celebration of the sacrament is good *for us*. Our role is to minister God's pardon and peace in a way that these gifts are clearly offered and can be accepted.

Some will enter the confessional simply to *get*: to *get forgiveness* and then to *get out*. When it is clear that an individual does not want to—or cannot—move beyond what we might consider the basics, let us respect that desire or inability and waste neither his time and energy nor ours. Instruction on the postconciliar theology and practice of the sacrament of reconciliation has a place, but seldom is it within the celebration of the sacrament. Trying to force a parishioner to confess the way we would prefer is not likely to encourage her to come to us to confess again.

In line with this, we should take advantage of the opportunities we do have to offer our parishioners some instruction on the theology and practice of sacramental reconciliation.

Adult religion or continuing education classes are not the only resources we have available in this regard. The regular cycles of readings in the Lectionary, for example, provide us with many examples and parables of God's love and forgiveness. Many of us preach well enough on what these readings tell us about God's approach to sinners, but we do not always go one step further and try to explain how that love and forgiveness are expressed and, hopefully, can be experienced, in the sacrament.

9. Do not minimize or trivialize the penitent's confession

Penitents are vulnerable. What they want to say—about what they have done, about themselves—is seldom easy, is often embarrassing, and is sometimes humiliating. We want to do all we can to make the situation easier and to put things in perspective.

Part of making the situation easier is taking what they are saying seriously—which means taking *them* seriously. In the first chapter I reported a conversation in which a penitent recounted her disappointment when she confessed something that was difficult to say, and then felt ignored by her confessor's not paying attention to something that was important to her. There are other examples:

He was single, in his early twenties. And he was confused. He was trying to figure out what he really wanted to do with his life at the end of this, his senior year. He was also beginning to get fed up with living in an environment that equated genital activity with "real" masculinity and assumed that a successful life had to include a successful sex life. "I'm all over the place on this, Father. I'm trying to turn my back on some of my past, but sometimes it seems like all I can think about are my past sexual experiences. I just can't seem to put them behind me."

"So you entertain impure thoughts and they keep entertaining you!" his confessor chuckled. The young student looked up at the priest—and got up and left. He later told a close friend that he knew the priest was just trying to be funny, was trying to take a little tension out of the moment. "But," he said, "I felt like he wasn't taking me seriously. This is important to me—and he started out by cracking a joke."

Again, our prior relationship with the penitent, if such exists, will be instrumental in suggesting our response. In some cases, humor such as the above attempt might be just the right thing. But in other cases, particularly when we do not know the person, and especially if the person is confessing behind the screen—a situation in which the all-important messages of facial expression, body language, and gestures are absent—resorting to humor can be hazardous.

Humor is not the issue. The issue is that our penitents, perhaps more than anything else, want us to take them seriously. What they confess is important *to them; they* know their difficulties, their hopes, their fears far better than we do. Penitents come to confession hoping to be offered forgiveness and peace, not to be entertained—and certainly not to have their assessment of themselves trivialized.

There are times, to be sure, when penitents do take themselves too seriously, when they are, in fact, making mountains where none should stand. *But the first step towards helping them put things in perspective is to meet them at their perspective*: to respect where they are now, before we try to lead them to what we think might be a better place.

10. Do not be too quick to offer definite answers to specific situations

Or, put positively, think twice—at least—before giving a *yes* or *no* to questions such as, "Father, should I do [this or that]?"

As mentioned earlier, sacramental confession ordinarily is neither the time nor the place for counseling or spiritual direction, but often it is the only opportunity for guidance that some parishioners will have or seek. Parishioners will come to confession and ask how they ought to go about dealing with a specific situation or with a specific person.

Sometimes we may be able to give a direct, easy answer but, unfortunately, that will not always be the case. Particularly complicated and sensitive are questions involving someone other than the penitent. These situations demand extra prudence, caution, and patience.

For example, a fourteen-year-old boy confesses he is sexually active, and in the course of his confession asks us if he should tell his parents. How are we going to answer his question? *Can* we answer his question with a simple yes or no?

This is obviously a serious situation, and from several perspectives. The boy is engaged in behavior the Church considers gravely wrong. He is obviously concerned about what he has done: he has overcome the embarrassment of confessing his sin, and has taken a step further by asking us for advice. Other concerns might be on his mind or on ours, such as the possibility of sexually transmitted diseases or the possibility and consequences of a pregnancy.

In addition to hearing his confession, what can we do? We will certainly want to acknowledge the "grace of the moment" that has brought him to the sacrament. We can affirm his courage in confessing his behavior. And we can support his thinking about getting some help with this situation.

After all, no fourteen-year-old has the resources, the experience, or the perspective to deal with a situation such as this alone. These are some of the things we can say and do. But what about his question, *Should I tell my parents?*

It would be ideal if our young penitent has an exemplary relationship with his parents, one characterized by all the right amounts of concern, understanding, challenge, and support. We may hope for that, but do we know if it is true in his case? The actual circumstances of his family life and relationships may fall far short of the ideal. Not a few parents will be psychologically and emotionally incapable of being "the ideal parents" here. Some may react with the silent treatment; others may express their anger, disappointment, and embarrassment with physical or emotional punishment. A few, sadly, might not really care at all. "Father, should I tell my parents?" We've said that we ask questions in the confessional in order to find out how we can minister more effectively to a penitent. So perhaps we shouldn't rush to answer our young penitent's question but, instead, ask him a question of our own:

- *Does your asking me mean you're not sure whether telling your parents is a good thing or not?*
- *What kind of relationship do you have with your parents? How do you think they would react?*
- *Are you afraid (not just nervous, hesitant, or embarrassed) to tell your parents?*
- *You've already taken a very important step by telling me about this. Are there other people you are able to talk about this with as well? Have you talked about this with anyone else?*

We are not encouraging our young penitent to practice deceit or cultivate a life of secrecy if we do not answer "yes" to his questions about telling his parents. I do believe, however, that unless we have some idea of what his home life is like, we should be cautious about offering a generic advice of either "yes" or "no." This young man will need someone to help him further address and manage his behavior. He has taken the first step by informing us. Perhaps others should know as well, and it may well be that those others would include his parents. But the way in which this information is presented, the time and the place, and the likely consequences of such a disclosure must also be considered. What might be good for James might not be as good—or may even be counterproductive—for John. My reflections here are not meant to promote deception but, rather, a careful discernment as to whom to tell, when, and how.

In discussing penances (chapter two, no. 4), we observed that the confession of some sins, e.g., gossip, slander, stealing, etc., call not only for contrition and a purpose of amendment, but also an attempt to repair the damage done or the possessions taken. In line with this, I offer here another example of the importance of our speaking with prudent reticence and hesitation about offering specific advice. It is one thing to advise a high school freshman, "Yes, you 'stole' this paper by presenting someone else's work as your own and you need to set the record straight with your teacher." It is quite another to counsel a fifty-year-old accountant that he should inform his supervisor that he has transferred a few hundred dollars of some clients' funds to his own account. It is clear that justice demands (and contrition implies) a return of the money or a rectifying of the accounts. But how that restitution should be done may not be as clear. Should he simply report his transgression to his supervisor in the hope that "all will be well"? In an ideal world, where sincere contrition and a firm purpose of amendment would set most things right, that would be fine. But our penitent doesn't live in that kind of world, and so a prudent consideration of the possibilities—and the consequences of those possibilities—is in order. Again, we don't know his supervisor or his company's policies. Advising him to self-report might mean his termination from the firm, with all of the consequent implications for income, family support, and reputation that would follow. If we cannot use any knowledge gained in the confessional to the detriment of the penitent, as canon 984 §1, prohibits us from doing, I do not think we can require a penitent to disclose such information to his detriment either. With reference to this example, that the penitent should make restitution is clear. Determining *how* that restitution might best be made is complicated.

In line with this, there will be situations in which a penitent asks us a question and we just don't know how to respond. It may be because the situation is unusually complex or, even for experienced confessors, perhaps it's the first time they have encountered such a situation. In cases such as this, we should not hesitate to say, "I don't know, let me think about it." As many confessors, counselors, and directors have learned from experience, it is usually better to offer no specific advice rather than offer some counsel unduly influenced by the pressure of the moment. (We can always suggest that the penitent return after we have had time to consider further the situation.) We can say, "In the meantime I will pray for you" in the hopes of offering some remedy to our ignorance!

If we are willing to give advice, we imply we are willing also to help him deal with the consequences. In situations such as these, it is all the more important to remember that the primary focus of the sacrament is the pronouncement of God's forgiveness. Other advantages that may come through the time in the confessional may be possible, but should be weighed carefully. Questions to discuss with the penitent (and here, a separate appointment might be in order) would include: how would you say it? What do you think their reaction will be? How will you deal with those consequences? And, of course, what are the consequences of *not* revealing the information?

In this and the previous chapter, I have offered a number of suggestions about "hearing confessions." I have discussed some things we should always keep in mind, some things we should take care to do and, especially in this chapter, some things we should take care not to do. These suggestions represent *a* way of hearing confessions: a way that, hopefully, will encourage seminarians and my brother priests to consider *their* way. Again, I do not claim my way is the only way or the better way. I encourage all of us to think carefully about our way in the light of what I have suggested. The goal is "better confessions": how to respond more directly, more effectively, to the people who come to our church seeking the word and the experience of God's pardon and peace.

In the next chapter, I will rely upon the guidelines I have suggested as I discuss hearing confessions for "certain people" or in "special situations."

CHAPTER FOUR

SPECIAL SITUATIONS, SPECIAL PEOPLE

Priests, penitents, and confessions come in a myriad of shapes and sizes, and it is precisely this reason why the "methodology" of hearing confessions cannot be blue-printed. There are people in particular situations, circumstances, or states of mind, however, to whom specific concerns or techniques often might apply. In this chapter I address some of these "particular situations," and offer some additional suggestions for practice.

1. Children

Many children come to confession well prepared. They have an understanding of the sacrament appropriate to their age, and they do not need much help in the "mechanics" of going to confession. Other children, however, leave us with the impression that they first heard about confession about a half-hour before they were told to "go in and do it." I addressed the need to prepare children for the sacrament in chapter two (point no. 6). I offer now some comments about celebrating the sacrament with children, whether they are well prepared or not.

First, I believe that children (I am talking about pre-adolescents) *can* sin and can realize that they have sinned. Anyone who has spent time in a grade school (or in a neighborhood) knows that children can hurt and wound each other with their sticks and stones and, yes, with their words. Part of this experience is growing up. And part of the sacrament is helping a child grow up to become more a *Christian* child and adolescent. While young children may not have a long list of "sins," children of most any age will know they have done things for which they should be sorry.

The standard fare of many children's confessions includes disobedience to parents and quarreling with siblings and friends. These are the "ordinary and daily sins" of childhood and the domestic scene. Seldom are they serious offenses, and there is ordinarily no need for us to treat them as such. But we can and should take a child's confession as seriously as we do the confessions of their elders.

Taking children seriously means beginning with them where they are and, when appropriate, trying to move them forward. With even a little encouragement, children often will be more forthcoming (and therefore more helpful in helping us help them) than many adults. Asking a child "a little bit more" about what he or she is confessing often will clearly suggest the way we might proceed. When a youngster admits to arguing with her brother or sister, for example, it might be helpful for us to ask if her sibling is older or younger than she is, and then ask how they usually treat each other. We might then follow with a question about what it is she likes most about her brother or sister. (Most children will come up with at least one good thing!) Then we might ask what she wants her brother or sister to like about her.

We do not ask these questions to pry. We are not out to uncover secret sins or "serious underlying problems." We are, again, trying to let them help us minister to them. We are trying to learn from them something about their lives that might give us an idea of what we might say or how best we might proceed.

As in the case with adults, what the child confesses—and what he tells us about himself or his situation—may suggest an appropriate penance. In the following example, the penance—arguably a "good penance"—comes from listening to, and asking about, what the child has confessed.

> *Ten-year-old penitent:* I fight a lot with my sister. She's always bugging me. I was pretty mean to her the other day, I wouldn't let her play with my Xbox. [*Confessor:* "Why not?"] She's got her own stuff and she's always wanting to use mine....Oh, and I stole a candy bar. I was with some friends and they dared me to do it.
>
> *Confessor:* [after talking about "charity" and stealing] For a penance—you're trying to do something to make up for what you're sorry for—why don't you take a dollar out of your allowance. That's about how much the candy bar cost, right? Take a dollar and buy something for your sister.

A penance of this sort (and our comments along with it) might be a small, though rich, treasure. First, we are encouraging the child to think about his relationship with his sister both in a practical way and in a way he is not used to thinking. Rather than thinking of her as "the one who is always going after my stuff," we are asking him to give her something. Second, we are asking him to make a small sacrifice to do that: an act that we can clearly indicate is related to what he took from someone else. This penance is a simple one and it deals with simple sins. But it also deals directly with this young boy and what he has confessed.

Another concern in hearing a child's confession is the *language* of the sacrament. The formula for sacramental absolution condenses a soteriological and Trinitarian statement, an ecclesiological petition to the Divine, and an authoritative statement of the sacramental power of orders into three brief sentences. I have often thought it a fine formula when absolving theologians and liturgists, but a bit unwieldy with most others. And I think it likely incomprehensible when our penitent is an eight-year-old boy or a ten-year-old girl.[1]

We work with what we have and what has been approved. We can, however, help children better understand the technical, adult language of the formula, and so not only forgive their sins but also promote their understanding and appreciation (and, hopefully, future practice) of the sacrament. We might "introduce" the formula of absolution, for example, and tell the child what it is we are about to say and why it is important. (In line with this, we may wish to review the *Rite's* Appendix II, Section IV, nos. 43–53, which provides a model of a non-sacramental communal penance service for children, and so offers prayers written with a child's level of understanding and experience in mind.)

2. The scrupulous penitent

Confessing a person suffering from scrupulosity can be as frustrating and painful for us as their "spiritual life" must be for them. In these cases I think it essential to return to that fundamental question: *Why is this person here?*

In the case of people who are scrupulous, the driving force is likely their fear of condemnation and the fires of hell. Both their fear and those fires are fueled by the way they think of God. God is for them more the prosecuting attorney driven to ferret out their offenses than he is the father joyfully welcoming his prodigal child back with a loving embrace.

There are many things we would like to tell a scrupulous person—things about God, things about themselves. We would like to tell them that God asks the impossible (perfection) of no one. We would like to tell them that they are good people who are trying to do the best they can. Most of all, perhaps, we would like to assure them that God does not have it in for them, and that they do not need to use the confessional as a place where yet another stay of eternal execution is granted them. At times we may be able to say some of that. But the chances are slim that, in the few minutes we have available, we will change the way she thinks of God or change the way she examines her conscience or goes to confession. We do what we can, when we can. And we make sure that, above all, we do no harm.

The last thing scrupulous penitents want to do is let themselves off the hook. It seems, in fact, that they will do everything possible to force the hook of God's accusation into their hearts all the more deeply. This is both symptom and result of the scrupulosity: terrified that they will forget or overlook a sin, they think the forgetting is itself a further sin. The scrupulous person is obsessed with examining his conscience, and his approach to the sacrament may itself be compulsive. Many priests have had the experience of hearing the same confession by the same person several times within a short time. The penitent returns again, one more time, to make certain that *everything* has been said, that *everything* has been understood and, above all, to make sure that *everything* was all right. The following are some suggestions to keep in mind when ministering the sacrament to people suffering from scrupulosity....

- Do not argue with them. Do not criticize the way they go to confession. We are not going to win and, more to the point, neither will they. Criticizing their scrupulosity will likely either give them more "matter" for their examination of conscience and next confession (they will think that now they're not even doing *that* right), or it will add yet another element of fear into their lives (now they must please not only God, but also us—if, in fact, they return to us).

- If we are asked whether a particular action is a sin, we should answer the question as directly and simply as possible. Many of us have been trained to respond to the question, "Father, is this a sin?" by discussing it with the person rather than by simply answering yes or no. The idea—ordinarily a fine one—is that we are encouraging our parishioner to assess her life as she knows and lives it, and thereby helping her develop an adult's responsibility in forming her conscience and her response to God's grace. But the scrupulous person wants to be accountable because God is her accountant, and the catalog of sins she is writing had better tally with the one God is keeping. If a scrupulous person asks *if* "this" is a sin and *if* it is not, we should say it is not. Attempts to address the penitent's scrupulosity are valuable and sometimes appropriate. Such addresses, however, are better done with brief, simple words of encouragement than with a lengthy question-and-answer approach that itself may resemble a legal hearing.

- Assign a penance that is as simple and as precisely defined as possible. "Do some act of charity for your spouse" or "spend a few minutes in prayer" may be an effective penance for some, but the scrupulous person may later wonder if the act he has in mind is enough, or how long it should last, or whether he needs to do it once or often, or what happens to his confession if he doesn't do it right, and "exactly how many minutes in prayer was that, Father?" If he returns to us for another confession, we may not remember the penance we assigned *but he will*—for, likely, his "mishandling" of his penance will be another sin he will want to confess.

- Consider asking penitents suffering from scrupulosity to say their penance immediately after you offer it to them. This can assure them that they have made a good confession, that their sins have been heard, that their penance has been said, and that God's forgiveness has been granted.

3. "Bless me, Father, but I have not sinned"

At times we will hear a confession in which, with respect to our discussion above, there seems to be no tendency towards scrupulosity whatsoever!

> Father, it's been two months since my last confession. I can't really think of any sins I've committed. Oh, I did miss my morning prayers two or three times.

A priest friend has told me that in such situations he's often been tempted to suggest, "How about the sin of pride?" He reports he's successfully resisted the temptation so far.

Few of us are able to go two days, let alone two months, without succumbing to temptations of any one of a number of daily, ordinary sins. Yes, it is likely this penitent has sinned. It is just as likely that she has not sinned grievously.

As in many confessions, we *need not* offer anything more than a penance and absolution, and in this instance that might be our preferred practice. Venial sins do not have to be confessed (although there is certainly value in doing so) and so we really shouldn't be concerned whether this woman has made a "good" (valid) confession. It is *her* confession. If she asks us for help in examining her conscience (which, in the example, she is *not* doing), we can assist her with that. But if her confession is pretty much as reported above and she seems content at leaving it at that, we will likely not do much good if we begin to suggest other sins she might consider. We may well think this penitent could benefit from an expanded examination of conscience, but providing a list of sins might not be the best way to do this. Perhaps the opposite strategy, where we concentrate on virtues rather than vices, might be more helpful—and appealing—to her:

- *It sounds as though you're really trying to live a good life. Let me make a suggestion to help you with that. What's one thing you'd really like to do better over the next month or so?*
- *It sounds as though you've done really well these past two months. Keep that up. And here's something more for you. Let's think of some virtues: charity, humility, patience…Which one of those would be good for you to pay some extra attention to over the next two months?*
- *It sounds as though you try to say your morning prayers as often as you can. What a wonderful practice! The next three times you pray, I'd like you to say an extra prayer for one of your neighbors—especially if it's someone you don't especially like. That person can benefit from your prayers too.*

4. The penitent who is "present in body but absent in spirit"

Ministering to those whom I call "present in body but absent in spirit" is also a difficult and often frustrating experience. I refer here to a not infrequent experience: adolescents who become penitents only because "confession" is part of their religious education program or, sometimes, because it is one of the requirements for their impending confirmation.

I refer to one occasion. I was one of several priests hearing the confessions of a class of high school sophomores and juniors. After a half-dozen "confessions," it was clear that whatever the caliber of the students' preparation for the sacrament of confirmation, they had little, if any, preparation for the sacrament they were supposed to be celebrating now. It is one thing to work with a penitent when she is confused about the "process" of confession or is uncertain how to proceed. But this was something different. These kids didn't know *anything*. They did not know what they were expected to do in confession or even why they were here sitting across from me. At one point I began asking my penitents if they understood why they were here and what we were about. The summary response was, "Sure, we were told we had to come in and talk with you so that we'd be able to get confirmed next month."

I have addressed above the importance of instruction and catechesis about the sacrament. Relevant to this situation, I offer what I consider to be an honest—the most honest—response in such a situation. I offered each young man or woman a chance to confess. I asked each one if they had anything they wanted to talk about. I also asked if they remembered doing anything for which they were sorry. To each who said "No, nothing," I concluded our time together not with the words of absolution but with a brief prayer asking God to bless them as they prepared to be confirmed. I explained to each one that I was not giving them absolution and we were not celebrating the sacrament of reconciliation because they had told me they had done nothing for which they needed to be forgiven. And, since they had been taught that their confirmation was their affirmation of their baptismal commitment (the operative theology of confirmation in that diocese), I offered each a simple suggestion or two as to how they might put into action what they were affirming by their words.

I am not entirely pleased with my approach in this situation. I know that I would be even less pleased had I just shrugged and done "sacramental business as usual." My thinking? Usually we think of pastoral decisions as those made in favor of the penitent. I thought the decision this time should be made in favor of the Church. I saw no reason to go through "sacramental motions," prolonging what was already an uninteresting time for them, and then conclude with the solemn formula of absolution in the hope that *ex opere operato* is better than nothing. Better to respect the integrity of the sacrament, I thought. And better hopefully to offer them (and, later, their teachers) a calm and clear message that what we are doing in this sacrament is serious business—which is why we are serious about doing it.

5. The penitent in need of counseling or psychotherapy

We experience limitations in our ministry of reconciliation. Sometimes we are limited by the time we have available for any one individual. At other times we feel at a disadvantage because we cannot address the person face-to-face. We may at times feel handicapped because we are not as conversant as we would like to be with psychological concepts or counseling techniques. And of course—necessarily—we are limited strictly by the seal of confession.

I have remarked several times that we are ministers *first* of God's pardon and peace. We offer that Divine Gift in our sacramental ministry more effectively than we can hope to offer "human solutions" to specific problems. The sacrament is primarily a time for God's promise of reconciliation to be announced, effected, and celebrated, rather than an occasion for in-depth counseling or crisis management. But, again, *confession* is the only opportunity for counseling or problem-solving that some people have available to them or of which they will take advantage.

We should not consider every major problem a parishioner brings to the sacrament as an occasion for referral to a professional counselor. But we must know when such is advisable. And we must know when it is appropriate to *suggest* that the penitent consider making an appointment to see us outside the confessional. The sins that lead to or result from serious marital or family problems can be forgiven through the sacrament. But the pain, hurt, and the psychological and emotional roots of these issues may need to be addressed through the counseling we or a professional can offer on a more regular and intense basis. A mid-life crisis or simply growing up can involve sins of envy and pride, against charity and chastity; but lengthy conversations as to "who I am and who I'm becoming" are discussed more effectively in the more relaxed (and often less time-limited) format allowed by spiritual direction. Certainly we deal with people as they are, where they are. We also try, when appropriate and necessary, to guide them into other helping relationships. *Why is this person here? From what does he or she need to be freed?* The better we can answer that question, the more we will be able to offer both God's grace and our human help to our parishioners.

Unless we have the benefit of specialized training, we cannot expect to be expert counselors or psychotherapists. But we are wise if we take some time to learn more about basic psychology, and about the basic forms of neuroses and psychoses. Workshops, seminars, and discussions with our colleagues can be a helpful supplement to our own study and reflection. Perhaps most important, we need to realize—and we need to be comfortable with—what we *don't* know. If we find ourselves wishing we had the skill to assist someone who presents us with a short-term or (especially) chronic problem, then it is probably appropriate that we at least encourage him to see us in our office and, perhaps, suggest the possibility that he seek professional help. The suggestion can be threatening to some, but to those truly in need of such help I think it will seldom come as a total surprise. People want to be told they are "okay." But when they are not: when they are truly suffering, or when they are a cause of suffering for others—when they are, in today's parlance, dysfunctional—they want to be told that the kind of help they need is available.

Telling a parishioner in confession that she needs "special help" need not, and must not, come across as an insult or an accusation. We are offering such advice because it is one way they might obtain the freedom and peace they seek.

> *I listen to what you're telling me, what you're saying. It sounds as though you feel you really need some help to deal with this. Maybe even some extra, special help. It sounds like you're frightened by all of this, frightened about what's going on in your life. Am I reading you the right way?*

Such a question "opens doors." It invites our penitent to talk about her life more. And it suggests that it is all right for her at least to consider whether she should seek "special help."

Let us take another example of where counseling is clearly required—and where the stakes are especially high:

"Father, I'm sorry, so very sorry. This is awful. I've been abusing my daughter. Physically. Sexually. She's twelve. I know that it's so terribly wrong, but I just can't seem to help it. I love her so much, and I don't want to hurt her. But it's, well, I just can't stop. She's all I've got in the world now...."

The tragic situation of child abuse. Were we psychologists, psychiatrists, social workers, physicians, or professional counselors, we would be required by law in most (if not all) states to notify the authorities of what we have been told. But this legal obligation does not—it cannot—bind us as confessors. Because we are bound by the seal of confession, we can say nothing about this to anyone at any time.

It is likely that whatever we can do for this man—and what we might be able to do for his daughter—we will be able to do only within the context of the sacrament. If we think it necessary to deal with him and his very real problem at greater length, we can suggest he return regularly to us in the confessional—or, perhaps, meet with us in our office. *If* we decide to encourage him to seek professional counseling, we must make sure he knows the difference between sacramental reconciliation and professional therapy. In line with this, we must explain that any professional he sees is required to report his abuse of his child to the authorities. It would be irresponsible on our part to direct him towards assistance in the external forum without informing him of the consequences.

A situation such as this is often as complicated to deal with as it is serious. Clearly, the gentleman needs professional help and we would like to help him obtain that help. Clearly, we are gravely concerned for the victim of the abuse. And clearly we want, above all, to do no harm—which, in this instance, means we do not want to "close doors." He has come to us seeking help. As we encourage him to take the next step and consider seeing a counselor, we must keep *our* door wide open. He may adamantly refuse to move the issue outside the confessional. His refusal would be most unfortunate. But what he is willing to do, at least at this time, is talk to us. Allowing him to continue to feel that he can talk with us may not resolve the situation. It may be, however, the only way he can and will talk about the matter—and therefore the only way of keeping alive the hope that in the future what needs to happen will happen.

In the above case, much needs to be done. Unfortunately, we cannot do it all. We attend to what is perhaps the one positive element: that the man is at least talking to us. And we do what we can to keep that conversation going.

6. "This isn't a sin, but..."

There are two occasions when we hear this statement. The first is the overly anxious or scrupulous penitent who doesn't think that she has committed a sin, but just wants to "make sure."

Why is this penitent here? As I have commented earlier, the scrupulous penitent likely views God as judge and accountant, and so she wants to make sure she doesn't owe anything. Discussions about moral theology and the primacy of conscience are unlikely to be helpful to her. What she wants is assurance that God is not holding anything against her. What we can offer, as mentioned in the above section dealing with scrupulous penitents, are words that clearly and unambiguously say to her, "I understand your concern; you can put these fears to rest."

"This isn't a sin, but..." A second occasion is more complex. It comes, not when we hear the confession of someone who is afraid, but, rather, of a parishioner who is struggling with Church teaching on one hand and his genuine, sincere assessment of his behavior on the other. Most often this will happen in the context of artificial birth control or a sexual (particularly a homosexual) relationship.

"Father, my wife and I practice birth control. I know what the Church teaches, but I really don't consider this a sin. We've talked about it a lot, and we believe we're responsible parents. We're trying to be. We have two children and we plan to have another, but the time just isn't right at the moment."

OR

"Father, I'm in a relationship with another woman. We've been living together for the past six months. I don't care what the Church says, it's a good relationship. We've both grown from it and it's made a real difference, a positive difference, in both our lives."

Both situations will be familiar to anyone involved in ministry today. In fact, we can say confidently that there are many more people involved in these situations than those who come to us wanting to talk about it! Many parishioners will not mention it in confession because they *don't* consider what they are doing to be wrong. Many others will simply stay away from the sacrament—and, unfortunately, from the Church.

But for those who do come: what kind of response can we offer? Realizing that we are ministers both *of* and *to* the Church, how do we see ourselves and our role in the sacrament? Do we see ourselves *only* as defenders of the Church and so stand up for Church teaching and argue? Do we see our primary role in such an encounter as teachers and thus try to persuade them, to "enlighten their conscience," as the saying goes? Or do we see ourselves primarily as "pastoral people," with the (faulty) understanding that as a "pastoral person" we can reassure them that as long as they're following their conscience, that's all we can ask of them and so send them on their way? In suggesting an approach, I again return to the principle, *Why is this person here?* What is he or she looking for? What do they hope to "get out of" this confession?

Precisely because many people won't even bother to bring their disagreement with Church teaching in a particular area to us, it is extremely important for us to answer the question, *Why is this person doing just that?*

One important thing to realize is that this person, unlike many others, has come to us in the sacrament. We assume, then, that they are looking for something. We can assume also that they are *not* looking for an emotional fight or an academic argument. Given the fact that they have come to us to talk (again, there are many others who do not bother to come), we might assume they are not looking for an "automatic acquittal," either. Based upon these assumptions, then, the following responses would be inappropriate:

> "Don't worry about it. You're doing just fine."
> "Well, as long as you follow your conscience, you're doing all right."
> "You're going against the teaching of the Church. You've got to stop."
> "Have you really read and studied *Humanae Vitae*?"
> "You're living in sin. I hope you're not receiving Communion."

What do the above statements do, other than firmly place us and the penitent in an "us *vs.* them" relationship on the one hand or, on the other, reduce us to the innocuous role of "support buddy"? The first two statements, for example, are weak because we are virtually abrogating our role as a minister *of* the Church: the Church who has called us to orders, and who has given us the opportunity, responsibility, and the authority to minister on its behalf. The third statement tells them only what they already know (they're not following the

Church's teaching), and abruptly demands they reverse a decision they have made apparently after serious thought and reflection. The fourth statement is only marginally better than the fifth: both tend to be arrogant and obnoxious—and both may well suggest that we are more interested in being distributors of documents and regulations than ministers who can begin where people are in the hopes of moving them further. We do want to teach, but we are to be *pastoral* teachers: teachers who can "lead the penitent with patience toward healing and full maturity."[2]

What, then, might we do? How might we respond? We recall two principles. First, answer that question, *"Why is **this** person here?"* (especially when others in their situation are not). Second, *allow them to help us minister to them; allow them to help us be a pastoral teacher to them.*

> *I hear you say that you and your wife want to take seriously your role as parents. Even more than that, because you're here, talking with me, I hear you say you want to be good Christian parents. And I hear you say you feel you're in a bind between what our Church teaches and how you think about that. What is it I can help you with here? Would you like to talk about the Church's teaching some other time, in another setting?*

What does a statement of this kind do? First, it acknowledges that we have heard them. Second, it honors a valuable principle in counseling of any sort: we acknowledge their strengths, we take note of what they consider their values ("You want to be good Christian parents"). Third, there is in the statement no trace of condemnation or judgment. Nor is there any indication that Church teaching is not important to us. Rather, the statement focuses first on them: on their situation, their decision, their life. Finally (yes, there is a lot said

101

in this short statement!), it is clear that we want to assist them *as their minister and as their teacher*.

Affirming that I accept our Church's teaching relevant to either of the above situations, I stress again that the essential thing to recognize in these examples is that *the people have come to the Church looking for something*. Unlike so many others in similar situations, they are not satisfied with a "don't ask and certainly don't tell" approach. Nor are they completely at ease with the situation they find themselves in. *If they were, they wouldn't have brought it up to us, nor would they have come to us in the first place*.

The people are here. Perhaps the best we can do is to treat them in such a way so that they will return. This means respect, understanding, and not looking upon this particular confession as the only or last chance we have to move them into conformity with the Church's teaching. If we keep the door open, if we see them as people in process and not as individuals who now, right now, must be "converted," we will have opportunities in the future to walk and work with them. And they will know that we are ready and willing to do that.[3]

7. Refusing/deferring absolution— sufficient purpose of amendment?

We discussed above the situation when a parishioner approaches the sacrament, albeit while experiencing some conflict with Church teaching. We consider a related case here: penitents whose "firm purpose of amendment" is in some doubt—either to us or to them.

The Code of Canon Law offers only two brief canons concerning the issue. Canon 980 states that "If the confessor has no doubt about the disposition of the penitent, and the penitent seeks absolution, absolution is to be neither refused nor deferred." Canon 987 echoes this from the perspective of the penitent: "To receive the salvific remedy of the sacrament of penance, a member of the Christian faithful must be disposed in such a way that, rejecting sins committed and having a purpose of amendment, the person is turned back to God." The "disposition of the penitent" referred to in canon 980 is the penitent's contrition for those sins committed, a contrition that includes, in the language of the second canon, a rejection of those sins committed and a purpose of amendment.

The notion of refusing absolution is distasteful to most, if not all, priests and understandably so. Dismissing penitents without absolution seems akin to slamming a door in their faces. Yet I have been asked, both in the seminary classroom and in conversations with brother priests, when and for what reasons absolution should or might be refused (better, *deferred*), and so the issue warrants some discussion here.

That a penitent approaches the confessional in the first place ordinarily indicates he is sorry for his sins and so rejects them, and this would ordinarily reflect his desire to amend his life and do better in the future. This seems clear in theory as well as in the vast majority of actual confessions. After all, who is pleased with the sins that he/she is confessing?

The questions that can arise, however—especially among new confessors—are, "How much contrition is sufficient? How firm should the purpose of amendment be? What if I, the confessor, or he, the penitent, is not sure about his ability to avoid this sin in the future?" Those asking these questions usually lack neither compassion nor good will. They are concerned for the integrity of the sacrament, and the laudable desire to avoid thinking of the sacrament as magic. And, as mentioned, penitents themselves sometimes doubt whether they have a sufficient purpose of amendment. This concern is seldom expressed in the canonical terminology of validity; it is more often a question, in the penitent's mind, as to whether she is making an "honest" confession. Many people do *not* want to "simply go through the motions," and they wonder about the value of confessing the "same old, same old" again and again.

The eminent moral theologian Bernard Häring has offered helpful insights on the matter of "assessing the purpose of amendment." His 1969 book, *Shalom: Peace—The Sacrament of Reconciliation*, is out-of-print, and so I reproduce here one of his reflections:

> In judging a penitent's purpose of amendment, the confessor would do well to keep in mind that even here the law of growth finds application. He will meet with some penitents who, while they are not scrupulous regarding the integrity of confession, are extremely precise regarding the statement of their resolution to amend. They might say, "Father, I cannot honestly promise that I'll never do this again. I still feel very much attached to it." It would be unfair immediately to conclude that such penitents have left the path of true sorrow. Very often, these are persons who are disturbed by the fact that their lower nature still craves satisfaction. They wish with their whole hearts that they could make the necessary promise, but their sincerity forbids it. They will not promise what they fear they cannot keep.
>
> St. Augustine faced similar problems with Christians who wanted in the most sincere way to give themselves over totally to God's will, but who recognized their own weakness. They would tell the saint, "God asks us to do what is impossible for us." Augustine resolved their doubts with the Gospel of the merciful Samaritan. He would tell them how the Samaritan brought the poor, beaten wayfarer to an inn and paid for the man's room, and how he recognized that this man, even after the care given him, would still need a period of recuperation: "Take care of him, and whatsoever you shall spend over and above, I, at my return, will repay you" (Lk. 10:35). So it is

with penitents. There are some who cannot rise immediately from their sickness, but need a longer cure before rising to full justice. Therefore Augustine would tell them (and he is quoted by the Council of Trent) to do what they could and pray hard for what they could not yet accomplish, because God does not ask the impossible of his creatures. There is no question of St. Augustine presuming that a short prayer always suffices to obtain a total change. He is trying to indicate that if a man is sincere, tries to do what he can, and at the same time prays, "Help me, O Lord, where my own freedom falls short," while he may not strictly be fulfilling the whole law, he is nonetheless, by his attitude, complying with God's command. For the moment, the Lord does not ask more from such a man.

I do not believe that one priest would ask another in confession to promise not to sin against fraternal charity in the future. Each knows how difficult this would be. Perhaps a saint could make such a promise. Yet, there are confessors who ask penitents living in difficult situations never to fall into a certain sin again. Some ask married people, for example, to vow or promise never again to yield to selfishness in the marriage act. Honest people will be hesitant about such a promise because they realize it may be impossible to keep. What the confessor might ask—it is only a matter of rephrasing—is that his penitent *try* not to commit this sin again.[4]

The Pontifical Council for the Family offered some guidelines regarding "sufficient amendment" in its 1997 document, "*Vademecum* for Confessors Concerning Some Aspects of the Morality of Conjugal Life" (reprinted in its entirety as Appendix I of this book). The document's title indicates its specific focus, but the principles and suggestions it offers are applicable to many confessional situations.

The third section of the document, "Pastoral Guidelines for Confessors," begins by offering four aspects confessors should keep in mind ("in dealing with penitents on the matter of responsible procreation"). It is the fourth aspect, "advice which inspires all, in a gradual way, to embrace the path of holiness," that is especially relevant here. The paragraph immediately following the "four aspects" reads:

> The minister of Reconciliation should always keep in mind that the sacrament has been instituted for men and women who are sinners. Therefore barring manifest proof to the contrary, he will receive the penitents who approach the confessional taking for granted their good will to be reconciled with the merciful God, a good will that is born, although in different degrees, of *a contrite and humbled heart*" (Ps 51:19).[5]

The document underscores the seriousness with which the sacrament must be approached, both on the part of the penitent and the confessor. Reconciliation is for those who are serious about their Christian life, a life that has demands and expectations:

> The confessor is bound to admonish penitents regarding objectively grave transgressions of God's law and to ensure that they truly desire absolution and God's pardon with the resolution to re-examine and correct their behavior. Frequent relapse into sins of contraception does not in itself constitute a motive for denying absolution; absolution cannot be imparted, however, in the absence of sufficient repentance or of the resolution not to fall again into sin.[6]

The *Vademecum* then spends several paragraphs in examining the cases of "subjectively invincible ignorance" and the pastoral "law of gradualness" (what Fr. Häring referred to as the "law of growth"), before offering what might be considered the bottom line when it comes to a confessor discerning whether a penitent's contrition and purpose of amendment is "sufficient":

> Sacramental absolution is not to be denied to those who, repen-
> tant after having gravely sinned against conjugal chastity,
> demonstrate the desire to strive to abstain from sinning again,
> notwithstanding relapses. In accordance with the approved
> doctrine and practice followed by the holy doctors and confes-
> sors with regard to habitual penitents, the confessor is to avoid
> demonstrating lack of trust either in the grace of God or in the
> dispositions of the penitent, by exacting humanly impossible
> absolute guarantees of an irreproachable future conduct.[7]

The confessor is to avoid demonstrating lack of trust either
in the grace of God or in the dispositions of the penitent, by
exacting humanly impossible absolute guarantees of an irreproachable future conduct. This is yet another application of
the fifth principle we discussed in chapter one: the priority of
God's word and action through the sacrament. If the
Kingdom of Heaven is like a mustard seed, than that seed
takes time to grow to maturity. No penitent approaching the
sacrament is taking the final exam in the spiritual life. He or
she is continuing to seek and, hopefully, continuing to
receive, the nourishment that will eventually bear fruit.

Most people who approach the sacrament today do so not
because they "have to," but because they want to. They want
some advice. They seek peace. They recognize their need for
forgiveness. We can take them where they are in the hopes of
helping them move onward and upward. As mentioned previously, we tend to move upward by a long and winding staircase, not by suddenly leaping from floor to floor.

8. Frequent devotional confessions

Many men and women who come frequently to the sacrament come confessing frequent, repeated, venial sins. These are
good people. Their lives seem to be in order. These are people
that often seem to us to be, in the best sense of the word, pious.

Why are these people here? Loneliness for some: they know that at least we will listen. Others continue to honor their religious education or family upbringing. Many elderly men and women (and elderly religious, in particular) were formed according to guidelines that called for frequent confession and a minute examination of the failure of one's duties in ordinary life. And for some, frequent confession is, quite properly, an important aid to their ongoing spiritual development. Even in the absence of grave sin, the appropriate and regular examination of one's conscience can be of great help in detecting patterns of weakness, imperfection, and apathy; bringing these matters to confession on a regular basis is one way some penitents remind themselves that the power of God's grace far exceeds their limitations. Father David Coffey offers a helpful insight on the value of regular devotional confessions, which he presents in the context of the relationship between baptism and reconciliation:

> Sin is forgiven in an instant, but pulling up the roots of sin, as an essential component of becoming conformed to Christ, is a process, the work of a lifetime. While baptism stands for the instantaneous and total victory of Christ over sin *for* each of us individually, penance, repeated as it is from time to time, stands for the process of the gradual appropriation of this victory *in* each of us, and not just penance as brought to bear on our grave lapses, but penance as burrowing ever deeper into our lives and gradually removing from them even the roots of sin, that is, penance as the practice of devotional confession. Hence the emphasis on perfecting the grace of baptism, conformity to Christ, heeding the Spirit, penance as sacrament and virtue taking root in life, and fervent, persevering service of God and neighbor....

Father Coffey observes that the practice of resubmitting

previously confessed (and absolved) sins should not be dismissed as a useless, overly pious exercise:

That the sentence of pardon is pronounced or repronounced in precisely this forum adds greatly to the power of the process of eradicating sin from our lives and thus becoming more perfectly conformed to Christ.[8]

Some have described listening to devotional confessions as being "stoned by popcorn." The expression may bear some humor, yet hopefully it would not be interpreted as condescending by those to whom it refers. While it may seem to some priests who have ministered as chaplains in a nursing home, an elderly day care center, or a religious community that some penitents may be stoning themselves needlessly by their detailed accounting of missed prayers, omitted acts of charity, distractions during one's daily devotions, and the like, it is important to remember that for others who make use of frequent or devotional confessions, the practice is, as Fr. Coffey suggests, "burrowing ever deeper into [their] lives and gradually removing from them even the roots of sin." Confession can be about the practice of daily conversion as much as it can be about the forgiveness of grave sins.

What can we offer these people? Remember the fundamental question: "Why is *this* penitent here?" Priests who minister to men and women in nursing homes or elderly day care centers should remember that these people have plenty of time to think about their past lives. As they address their faults, we might ask them to consider some of the things in their life of which they are proud. Then we may help place those happy memories in the context of God's grace to them, and suggest this as a reason and an occasion for their daily prayer.

Priests who minister regularly to religious communities would do well to acquaint themselves with the community's rule or customary behavior, at least to the extent that they can refer directly (and in the community's terminology) to values the particular community holds dear. For example, a chaplain ministering to a women's Benedictine community might "prepare" for hearing confessions by remembering that one guiding principle of the Benedictine way of life is *ora et labora* (prayer and work). Furthermore, even a brief reading of the Prologue of Benedict's *Rule for Monks* would offer him several ideas or themes he might call upon as he offers comments to his penitents or assigns their penance. Similarly, "preparing" to hear confessions at a nursing home may mean spending a few moments reflecting on why even the elderly and the sick are important members of the Church. The fruit of our reflections can suggest an appropriate comment or penance—or even a different attitude on our part—that we may wish to offer.

Finally, characteristic of many devotional confessions is the penitent concluding with a phrase expressing sorrow and asking forgiveness "for these and all the sins of my past life." This traditional Catholic phrase seems not to be as familiar to our younger priests as it is to those of my generation and before, and several times I've been asked if in cases such as this the penitent is trying to "slip something in."

Ordinarily, no, the penitent is not trying to slip something in. And, except for those suffering from scrupulosity, the phrase most likely is *not* expressing some doubt that one's past sins have been forgiven or confessed. Usually it is simply a straightforward expression of continuing contrition and purpose of amendment. It is the way that previous generations of Catholics were taught to conclude their confession.

Do these past sins *need* to be confessed? Sacramentally, no. But, as the above quote from Fr. Coffey suggests, there can be psychological, emotional, and spiritual benefits to confessing these sins once again. Some people may still feel the emotional or psychological weight of some specific sins in the past, and their repeated admission of them (even in a general way) may be their continuing efforts to express their sorrow. Others are simply following the way they have been taught to confess. My experience is that there is seldom any need to ask them to specify which sins in their past life they are referring to, but to accept the statement as the way they have been taught to confess, the way they are accustomed to confess, and the way they are comfortable confessing.

9. The penitent returning after a long absence

In chapter three (point no. 4) I offered one example of when a response on the confessor's part is not only appropriate but desirable. I offer a second example here.

A parishioner returning to the sacrament after a long absence will likely bring a wide range of emotions. In addition to being nervous because she may not know "how this is done anymore," she may be anxious as to what our reaction to her extended absence from the sacrament will be. And she may fear that her prolonged absence from the sacrament will require a difficult, detailed examination of the past years so that "all the sins will be covered" (or "uncovered," as the case may be!).

Before we assist her with whatever examination may be needed, it is important that we acknowledge what is *the* most important thing *at that moment*: that she is returning to the sacrament and to her Church. We can offer a simple yet sincere statement that not only acknowledges this as an important time in her life, but one that also softens an atmosphere that may be tense, confused, and fearful.

You say you've been away from the Church for six years. And now you're here today. Welcome back. I'm glad you're here. And may I ask: After such a long time away, **what brings you to the sacrament now?**

The closing question is an important one. She may tell us that her return is another step in her ongoing conversion. Or our question may encourage her to confess not only her sin, but what has happened in her life that has led her to resume a practice of which she has grown unaccustomed. Many people turn instinctively to the Church when a personal tragedy strikes. If such is the reason she has come to the sacrament, we should remember that while the sacrament is ordinarily neither the time nor the place for lengthy spiritual direction or counseling, *it may be the only counseling many will seek or receive.*

A final word about an individual returning to the sacrament after an extended absence. The question, *What brings you back to the sacrament now?* can be one of those "door openers." Similarly, we may consider asking the related question, *What kept (or drove) you away?*

If we ask this question, we should be prepared to hear from some parishioners that what drove or kept them away was, sadly, their confessor. The reasons offered will vary. Sometimes it will seem from their description that a confessor acted unwisely or unjustly. At other times it may appear that an unfortunate but innocent misunderstanding transpired. Whatever the reason (and discerning the truth may be difficult), common sense suggests that we take special pains not to repeat the offense. If a misunderstood or inappropriate question by a previous confessor contributed to the long absence, we should assure that whatever questions we ask are as necessary as they are respectful and prudent.

When a penitent returns after a long absence, there is reason both to celebrate and to be careful. We can certainly commend him for his courage in returning. And, if it seems that an injustice on the part of the confessor *was* done that long time ago—such has happened—*let us apologize.* If a minister of the Church has wounded, it is appropriate that a minister of the Church contribute to the healing of that wound.

10. "But I just can't go to confession"

Canon 960 states that "Individual and integral confession and absolution constitute the only ordinary means by which a member of the faithful conscious of grave sin is reconciled with God and the Church," and that "Only physical or moral impossibility excuses from confession of this type."

Occasionally someone will tell us—often in the church parking lot or at a rehearsal dinner!—that they "just can't" go to confession. Sadly, some people do have understandable reasons for having an aversion to the confessional. Some may feel they were treated harshly by a confessor. Others may have felt, or fear now, that they will be asked unnecessary and embarrassing questions. A few may have heard "horror stories" from their friends.

Not all of the "I just can't confess" situations can be attributed to perceived or actual poor pastoral form, however. One person will be firmly convinced he *has* committed the unpardonable sin. Another may feel so embarrassed by what she has done that she cannot even imagine putting it into words and acknowledging it to another. A parishioner who has been away from the Church for a long time may simply feel overwhelmed and just not know where to start. And even though our current *Rite of Penance* was promulgated in 1973, some people are still confused about the "mechanics" of confessing.

Ongoing ways of addressing these situations include our

preaching about the sacrament, as well as the other opportunities for catechesis that come our way. We are asked to speak "about something" on many occasions and at many gatherings, and I have found that neither interest nor questions are lacking when reconciliation is the topic. When working with adult classes (whether these be RCIA or continuing education), a carefully constructed and rehearsed "role play" confession, followed by discussion, can offer as much reassurance to the fearful as it can information to the confused.

Our immediate response to individuals who tell us they "just can't go to confession"? We might tell them that it seems they are trying to take a first step simply by sharing their difficulty with us. Other helpful questions on our part:

- *Can you at least tell me why you can't go to confession? What's the most difficult part for you?*
- *What can I do to help you? Would you like me to ask some questions—or is it the questions you think I might ask that is part of the difficulty?*
- *It's clear this bothers you. I respect that. Maybe we can do it this way: let's take it step by step, only as much as you can. What* **can** *you confess right now? What* **can** *you say?*

Situations such as these reflect the fifth principle I offered in chapter 1: that we have faith in God's word, and that if we are faithful in planting the seeds, God will give the growth. Our patient approach might help the parishioner confess now after all, or it may be one of the small paving stones in the sidewalk that will eventually lead them to celebrating the sacrament.

As for those who do manage to overcome their difficulty and eventually confess, my experience is that their confession does not sound as bad to our ears as it has resounded painfully in their hearts. If that is the case, our response should *not* be,

"Well, that wasn't all that bad, I've heard worse." Although no priest would intentionally belittle a penitent's confession, such a comment could be interpreted as such. Again, we do well to remember that a penitent's confession is always significant to him. More appropriate comments would focus, again, on the "grace of the moment": the courage the penitent displayed in confessing, the humility that led to the confession, and the freedom the penitent now enjoys.

11. The penitent who is a brother priest

Most priests consider their role as confessor as among the most important and fulfilling aspects of their sacramental ministry. My experience, however, is that no small number of priests approach the sacrament "as those confessing" infrequently. No doubt one reason for this is that it is embarrassing and humbling to admit our sins and failings to another. Since many of our parishioners find themselves in the same situation, this is a good thing for us to remember! But perhaps we feel the embarrassment more acutely, since we're admitting to a brother priest—often one with whom we live or work, or someone whom we know will see us later exercising our ministry—that we do not always live what we preach. Nevertheless, it is important to remember that to be a "good confessor," it is essential to be a "good penitent" as well.[9]

From the opposite perspective, I have heard priests remark that, when a brother priest asks them to hear their confession they feel honored, but also somewhat ill at ease. Sometimes the unease comes from the realization that our brother priest wishes to celebrate a sacrament that perhaps we ourselves have shied away from for too long. In these instances, our discomfort may be a graced reminder that we, too, can and should find ourselves celebrating the sacrament "on both sides of the screen."

At other times, however, the unease comes from a curious feeling of inadequacy or embarrassment. A young priest told me that he had agreed to be a regular confessor for a neighboring pastor but that he was "on edge" about it all. "What can I possibly tell him that he doesn't already know? *He's* been ordained longer than I have!" Other comments I have heard express much the same sentiment: "How can I give him advice? He's a much better (holier, more intelligent) priest (counselor, director) than I am!"

What can I possibly tell him that he doesn't already know? I can best address this question by reflecting upon what it is I am looking for—and what it is I am not—when I celebrate the sacrament as the one confessing. I recall an experience some years ago:

I had been on a rather lengthy round of substitute parish assignments, retreats, and days of recollection, and so had been away from my community (and my regular confessor) for some time. I realized I would soon be filling a brief assignment in the city where a good friend, a layman, lived. I wanted to celebrate the sacrament, and I wanted to celebrate it "well." Some of my past experiences on the other side of the screen have encouraged me not to confess to just "any priest," and so I asked my friend if he would make an appointment for me with a priest whom he knew would be "good."

My friend contacted a priest he knew well. The priest was only too happy to meet with me—until my friend casually mentioned I had a degree in sacramental theology. "Oh, Lord," was the priest's response. "He teaches reconciliation and *I'm* supposed to hear *his* confession? I hope I don't make a fool out of myself. Thanks a lot for getting me into this mess!"

My friend good-naturedly reported the priest's reaction to me, and I chuckled. "I know what he's feeling," I thought. He doesn't see an "ordinary guy" coming for confession; he sees a priest who has heard confessions, a theologian who has lectured and written about the history, theology, and pastoral practice of reconciliation, and maybe even a liturgist who actually wants to, gulp, *celebrate* the sacrament (!). I suppose it's roughly analogous to having your doctor ask you for advice on *his* diet.

The situation: a brother priest approaches, asking to celebrate the sacrament. *The dilemma*: what can we tell him that he doesn't already know, or that he himself hasn't told countless others so many times when he's been their minister? *A reflection*: maybe we won't be able to teach him anything new or profound. But maybe there's no need to "teach" him anything. Maybe he, this brother priest, just needs to hear those words—the words of God's love and forgiveness, and the Church's words of pardon and peace—he has offered to so many others so many times. Maybe he needs to hear his Church, "his priest," offer those words to him.

Remember: when I ask a brother priest to hear my confession, I am not expecting, nor am I asking for, a theological commentary on the sacrament. I am asking you to help me experience the Lord's peace, just as I try to help others experience that grace. Help me to believe that I am not a hypocrite because I preach the gospel better than I live it. Help me to know that my confession is one way I have chosen to try to be more accountable to God, to our Church, and to those to whom I minister. Remind me—show me—that I am a minister who also needs a minister. Be the Christ of God's grace to me as I so often try to be him to others. To put it simply: do not feel that you must impress me with a brilliant insight into the sacrament or a shrewd intuition into my own life. (Although I would welcome that, if it is there!) If I were looking for *knowledge about the sacrament* I'd read a book or enroll in a seminar. But I am looking for *the pardon and peace the sacrament offers.*

So be a minister, a priest, to me. Tell me those words of understanding and pardon that I offer to others—tell me that those words of grace—are meant also for me.

12. Communal penance services

Many parishes or parish clusters offer the "Rite for Reconciliation of Several Penitents with Individual Confession and Absolution" (hereafter referred to as "communal penance services" or "Rite II") each year, most usually during Lent and Advent. In fact, communal penance services may be the most frequent experience of sacramental reconciliation for many Catholics today. When thoughtfully prepared and carried out, the value of these communal celebrations is clear:

> [This form] of celebration, precisely by its specific dimension, highlights certain aspects of great importance: the word of God listened to in common has a remarkable effect as compared to its individual reading, and better emphasizes the ecclesial character of conversion and reconciliation. It is particularly meaningful at various seasons of the liturgical year and in connection with events of special pastoral importance.[10]

If the value of these celebrations is clear, clear also are the unique demands they make upon us as confessors. Faced with a line of penitents a dozen or more deep and conscious that the clock is ticking, we may well feel that we and our brother priests are mechanics on a sacramental assembly line. That impression, of course, is exactly what we should not want to give, no matter the number seeking to celebrate the sacrament that evening. What steps might we take to avoid giving this impression?

Before attending to this, it is important to address several misunderstandings and unacceptable practices sometimes associated with Rite II. First, Rite II is not Rite III (General

Absolution), nor should it be presented as such. Canon Law is clear as to when General Absolution is permitted (canons 960–963), and our bishops have stated that the conditions allowing General Absolution ordinarily do not exist or occur in this country. The USCCB has also clarified that the following practices that have been incorporated in some places over the past years for Rite II celebrations are not allowed: penitents are *not* to be instructed to confess "just one sin"; a common penance is *not* to be given, if this would entirely replace an individually-given penance; absolution is *not* to be given to the assembled community, thus replacing the absolution given to each individual penitent.[11]

These practices seem to have been introduced because some believe that, first, they emphasize the communal and social nature of sin and reconciliation and, second, they save time at communal celebrations. If these are indeed the motives underlying these practices, they are understandable to some extent. In addition to being prohibited they are also, I think, misguided, for they ultimately undercut and defeat what it is we are trying to promote: the value and significance of the personal nature of the sacrament. Emphasizing the communal nature of sin and forgiveness is laudable; it can be accomplished far more effectively (and lawfully) by selecting appropriate readings, delivering a suitable homily, and offering a pertinent examination of conscience. More to the point, not one of us would visit physicians who would direct us to tell them "just one thing" that is hurting or bothering us. Nor would we trust physicians whose proffered remedy or prescription is the same for each and every one of their patients. Finally, I fail to see the value in moving the "climax" of the sacramental celebration—the pronouncement of the Lord's merciful forgiveness—away from that personal encounter between priest and parishioner and placing it in a generic setting. I began the introduction to this book by writing that celebrating the sacrament of reconciliation is among the most significant and personal encounters we priests can and will have with our parishioners. Therein lies a good part of its value, which is not served at all by practicing it in a way that suggests a "one-size-fits-all" mentality. The goal of our sacramental ministry in the confessional, whether the sacrament be celebrated according to Rite I or Rite II, is not to set records for confessions heard and absolutions given. It is to minister as effectively and personally as we can, in the time available, to whomever approaches us. The confessions at a communal penance service may have to be shorter, but that does not mean that the personal nature of the sacrament should be set aside.

How, then, faced with a crowd, can we best try to do what is possible? I offer the following suggestions:

a) Whether advertised in the parish bulletin or through remarks during the Eucharist the preceding Sundays, parishioners should have a clear understanding of what a communal reconciliation service is and what it is not. It is *not* general absolution; it *is* individual confession and absolution. It is fine (and wise) to state that this opportunity for reconciliation is usually not the time nor the place to present the priest with complicated problems and issues; it is something else to say that "the priest won't say anything at all, he's just there to listen." (At the risk of overstating my concern here, I ask again: why would we want to abrogate so much of the potential of our ministry by taking a temporary vow of silence?)

b) The very structure of a communal penance service often militates against the proper practice of the individual interchange between priest and penitent. Fr. David Coffey has described the difficulty well:

> One of the weaknesses and disappointments of [Rite II] is that when it is carried out in a normal parish congregation, it is well nigh impossible to persuade the people to remain to the end....People will stay to make their confession and pray their penance, but then they leave. They cannot face the prospect of remaining in the church with nothing to do (but pray!) for an indeterminate period until all the confessions have been heard.[12]

I agree with Fr. Coffey that the ideal would be to celebrate the rite as it is envisioned: that, in addition to a communal celebration of the word, a homily, and collective examination of conscience preceding individual confession and absolution, the congregation would also participate in a communal thanksgiving afterwards. I also agree with him that this ideal is far more likely to be both practical and effective in seminaries and retreat houses rather than in the typical parish. In light of this, it would seem preferable that we help ourselves and our people by inviting them to stay after their individual confessions "for a time," but not insisting upon a definite conclusion to the rite, thus allowing priest and penitents alike to attend to their individual encounters with less of a preoccupation about keeping others waiting. Again, it is true that some of the communal nature and the communal significance of what Rite II attempts to offer would be lost by such a practice. This would call for an even clearer presentation of these communal aspects in the choice of the reading, the homily, and the collective examination of conscience. It is a far from perfect situation, but the curtailment of the collective conclusion would seem to be one of the adaptations that the *Rite of Penance* allows priests to make for pastoral reasons.[13] Some parishioners, of course, will be willing and able to linger after their individual confessions. Hopefully our musicians can continue to provide a reflective atmosphere in the church for them. Perhaps a vestige of the "communal nature" might be offered, in the form of some light refreshments, to those usually inclined to simply confess and go.

c) As with all confessions, we may not know what will be confessed but we can still prepare ourselves for the celebration. Taking the trouble to find out the reading ahead of time might allow us to shape some brief yet to-the-point remarks we might offer to those parishioners whose confessions are relatively simple and straightforward. Similarly, paying attention to the homily may allow us to reinforce the message offered there. Such comments on our part will obviously add to the length of the evening, but they need not do so excessively. Reflected upon beforehand, even a sixty-second (or less) offering on our part can offer some thoughts worthwhile for our parishioners, and if we have some general comments in mind we can certainly adapt them as appropriate to each parishioner. Some suggestions for such comments can be found in chapter 2 ("Some things to consider," no. 2).

d) Even when grave sins are confessed during a Rite II celebration, counsel can be given that is as encouraging and helpful as it is succinct:

> Father, I know we don't have a whole lot of time to talk about this. But, well, I'm married …and I have been having an affair for the past couple of months.
>
> *The first thing I want to tell you is that you're showing me a lot of humility and courage right now. I want to commend you on that. That is so important. The second thing I want to tell you is that I will give you absolution. You are sorry, that is clear, and this is your chance to get back on track. The third thing: please feel welcome to come back to me or another priest and talk about this when we do have more time. We'll be willing to help you any way we can.*

Referring again to the fifth principle we discussed in chapter one, we may not be able to "do it all" in *this* confession. But we can plant some seeds to make a subsequent confession possible.

e) Most communal penance celebrations are held during Advent and Lent. A helpful comment or question during December might be along the lines of, "Do you have a New Year's resolution yet? Is there one thing you could do that would make next year better for you (your family, your spouse) than this year was?" In those few weeks before Easter, a few words of encouragement to attend and participate in one or more of the Triduum liturgies might be appropriate.

f) Finally, I offer several readings (along with a homiletic suggestion or focus) I believe are particularly appropriate for communal reconciliation services. The first two readings, from the Old Testament, deal specifically with the communal nature and effects of sin. The two New Testament readings present the "personal" effects of sin in a way that many parishioners do not often think about. All four readings are familiar to our parishioners, yet they are readings about which they seldom hear us preach. Perhaps "fresh" homilies about these familiar readings might provide some new insights about sin—and the power of the sacrament.

- *Genesis 4:1–11.* The account of Cain and Abel is certainly familiar, as is Cain's memorable question, "Am I my brother's keeper?" A fresh approach to this passage would have us suggesting that God's answer to Cain's question is, in fact, "NO." Cain is not his brother's keeper, in that animals in zoos and bees in hives have keepers, whereas humans have brothers and sisters, and it is precisely in this relationship that Cain has failed![14]

- *Genesis 11:1–9.* John Paul II comments upon this account of the building of the tower at Babel at some length in his *Reconciliation and Penance*, pars. 13–15. He believes "that the tragedy of humanity today, as indeed of every period in history, consists precisely in its similarity to the experience of Babel" (par. 13). The document is out of print, but may be accessed through the Vatican's website. The following quote indicates the direction of the Pope's comments:

  Why did the ambitious project fail? Why did "the builders labor in vain"? They failed because they had set up as a sign and guarantee of the unity they desired a work of their own hands alone, and had forgotten the action of the Lord. They had attended only to the horizontal dimension of work and social life, forgetting the vertical dimension by which they would have been rooted in God, their Creator and Lord, and would have been directed towards him as the ultimate goal of their progress (par. 13).

- *Mark 10:46–52.* The disciples finally bring the noisy, insistent beggar Bartimaeus to Jesus. "Son of David, have mercy on me!" is Bartimaeus' plea. Jesus' response goes right to his heart: "What do you want me to do for you?" Approaching the sacrament of reconciliation, Jesus asks us the same question: "What is it you want me to do for you?" What is our answer?
- *John 1:1–44.* The account of Jesus raising Lazarus from the dead is proclaimed on the Fifth Sunday of Lent in the "B" Cycle (and may be proclaimed as that Sunday's gospel each year). It's reference to Jesus' resurrection from the dead. His promise of

eternal life is clear, but a powerful image of the sacrament of reconciliation is offered in the last line, as Jesus says, "Unbind him, and let him go." How have our sins bound us? How could our lives be better if we let Jesus set us free?

Concluding Remarks

The danger of writing a handbook for sacramental reconciliation is that such a book could suggest that a priest's ministry in the confessional depends largely upon mastering a series of techniques. As I said in the introduction, however, this book cannot provide a blueprint or flow chart for confessors. But *A Confessor's Handbook* can encourage priests and seminarians to *consider* the experience of reconciliation: to consider the different reasons people approach the sacrament (why is this penitent here?) and to consider the possible ways of responding to a particular penitent (from what does this person need to be freed?), and so engage the penitent in a dialogue that is truly pastoral and sacramental.

How long should a confession last? What needs to happen in the confession? What, exactly, should you do when you encounter *this* kind of situation? No book can answer these questions. A confession should last as long as it needs to last. What should take place in the sacrament is what needs to take place. And there are usually several effective ways to respond to any given situation. This book offers *a* measure of comparison, *a* reference point by which others can reflect upon and assess their confessional practice.

As we proceed with that reflection and assessment, we should never forget the utterly *sacred* nature of what it is we are doing when we serve as ministers of the sacrament. Today's society offers and promotes countless ways by which men and women can deal with their fears, anxieties, sins, and guilt: counselors, therapists, and psychiatrists; group sessions, encounters, and workshops. Many of these individuals and events do contribute toward a holy and healthy humanity, and there are similarities, to be sure, between what they offer and what can occur in the sacrament of reconciliation. Yet, the sacrament of reconciliation—and our ministry as confessors—is unique:

> We do not want to be psychotherapists in the confessional. This is not our job and would merely be silly charlatanism. We must simply be priests, but that wholly. We lend historical tangibility to God's effectively forgiving word in a personal happening; we are not applying magical machinery. We should even know when to regard a penitent as a patient for a psychotherapist and send him to one. *But we possess one word which no psychotherapist can say: the word of God which forgives sin.* The psychotherapist says a word which is meant to cure illness; *we say a word which forgives sin in God's sight.* Even if we cannot remove the illness—heavy burden though it is in many cases—*we can, however, take away the death in illness, the despair in it and the guilt.*[1]

It is God's loving grace that moves men and women to acknowledge their sin and to approach the sacrament in which and through which the forgiveness of that sin is effected and expressed. The power of the sacrament is the power of Christ; he is the primary minister—*Christus auctor sacramentorum*, as Saint Ambrose said. But, as ministers of the sacrament, we are more than liturgical presiders or verbal disseminators of pardon. To the extent that we take penitents' confessions seriously—which means fully accrediting and respecting the courage, honesty, humility, and seriousness of conversion with which they approach the sacrament—to that extent can we be a true *instrument* of the sacrament, an ambassador of God's peace, and a sacrament ourselves of

God's love most excellently manifested in the primordial sacrament of his Son:

> [T]he priest, as the minister of Penance, acts "in persona Christi." The Christ whom he makes present and who accomplishes the mystery of the forgiveness of sins is the Christ who appears as the *brother of man*, the merciful High Priest, faithful and compassionate, the Shepherd intent on finding the lost sheep, the Physician who heals and comforts, the one Master who teaches the truth and reveals the ways of God, the Judge of the living and the dead, who judges according to the truth and not according to appearances.[2]

Furthermore, the ultimate effectiveness of a priest's ministry—be it sacramental, pastoral, or even administrative—is never measured entirely by how well one knows "what to do." A priest can master the history, theology, and even the ritual actions of the Eucharist and still be an "ineffective celebrant." This disparity between "doing" and "being" is even more true in the celebration of sacramental reconciliation, the sacrament that many times requires the priest to "show himself" to an extent far greater than is expected or called for in the other liturgies of our Church. The effective confessor is not the priest who has mastered the techniques, or who is well versed in human psychology, or who knows what to say or what to do on every occasion. The effective confessor, ultimately, is the credible confessor.

A confessor is credible when he knows from his own experience as penitent the fear and the courage with which his people approach the sacrament. He is credible because he has experienced, with another minister, both the embarrassment of his sin and the gift of God's grace. Whatever he may have learned about human behavior and the art of counseling certainly will help him help his penitents. But he will continue becoming an effective *and* credible confessor to the degree that he knows what it is to confess to another and to have another minister to him. Professional competence can support and strengthen our personal credibility. Seldom can it replace it.

The challenge of the priesthood is to allow Christ and his power to be present as visibly and tangibly as possible, so that Christ may accomplish what the Father sent him to do. My hope is that the principles, suggestions, and recommendations I have offered in this book will assist my brother priests (and those preparing for the priesthood) in becoming effective instruments of God's pardon and peace. My book will have served its purpose if it simply allows us pause for a moment, that we might reflect upon how we minister this sacrament of peace now—and how we might better embrace our ministry of reconciliation in the future.

NOTES

Chapter One

1. James D. Davidson, et al., *The Search for Common Ground: What Unites and Divides Catholic Americans.* (Huntington, IN: Our Sunday Visitor Books, 1997), p. 26. The figure "one-fifth" reflects *registered* parishioners—that is, about 66 percent of all who identify themselves as Catholic. I am grateful to Dr. Davidson for his offering me a further breakdown of his study. The following statistics represent the confessional practice of *all* Catholics (registered and nonregistered) at the time of the study (1995): once a month or more, 8 percent; several times a year, 11 percent; one or two times a year, 24 percent; never or almost never, 57.

2. A study by the Center for Applied Research in the Apostolate (CARA) shows similar statistics for the years 2005 and 2008: "Three quarters of Catholics report that they never participate in the sacrament of Reconciliation or that they do so less than once a year....About one in eight Catholics (12 percent) participate in Reconciliation once a year and an identical proportion do so several times a year. Two percent report that they participate in Reconciliation at least once a month." "Catholic Data, Catholic Statistics, Catholic Research," URL: http://www.cara.georgetown.edu/bulletin/index.htm © CARA 2009.

3. Gerard T. Broccolo, "The Minister of Penance," in *The New Rite of Penance: Background Catechesis* (Pevely, MO: St. Pius X Abbey, 1975), 50.

4. *Catechism of the Catholic Church*, ET for the United States of America copyright ©1994, United States Catholic Conference, Inc.—Libreria Editrice Vaticana, par. 1548.

5. John Paul II, *Reconciliation and Penance*, Post-Synodal Apostolic Exhortation, 2 December 1984, par. 29.

6. *Catechism*, par. 1466.

7. *Reflections on the Sacrament of Penance in Catholic Life Today: A Study Document* (Washington, DC: United States Catholic Conference, Inc., 1990), reports that "Priests themselves indicated that they think they need more training or help to function more effectively as confessors, particularly with regard to the possibilities for moral and spiritual dialogue created by the revised rites of penance" (p. 26).

8. John Paul II, *Reconciliation and Penance*, par. 32, emphasis mine.

9. USCC, *Reflections on the Sacrament*, p. 20.

10. Karl Rahner, "Problems Concerning Confession," in *Theological Investigations III: The Theology of the Spiritual Life*, trans. Karl-H. and Boniface Kruger (New York: Seabury, 1967), p. 201. In context, Fr. Rahner is speaking of questions designed to "dissect" the penitent's confession so as to add "matter" that the penitent is either unaware of or is deliberately withholding. Such motivation Fr. Rahner condemns by virtue of its "lack of tact…curious questioning…attitude of suspicious distrust…kind of spying attitude" (p. 202). It is clear later in his article that Fr. Rahner equally disapproves of a confessor who merely "goes through the motions" in such a way that the penitent is not sure he or she is being taken seriously (see the quotation cited by note 11, below).

11. Canon 960: "Individual and integral confession and absolution constitute the only ordinary way by which the faithful who are conscious of serious sin are reconciled with God and the Church. Only physical or moral impossibility excuses from this kind of confession, in which case there also may be reconciliation in other ways."

12. Rahner, "Problems Concerning Confession," p. 205.

13. USCC, *Reflections on the Sacrament*, p. 6.

14. USCC, *Reflections on the Sacrament*, pp. 8–9.

Chapter Two

1. *Rite of Penance*, Introduction, no. 6-b.

2. *Rite of Penance*, Introduction, no. 18.

3. *Catechism*, par. 1459.

4. John Paul II, *Reconciliation and Penance*, par. 31.

5. *Rite of Penance*, Introduction, no. 18. The text continues: "This act of penance may suitably take the form of prayer, self-denial, and especially service to neighbor and works of mercy. These will underline the fact that sin and its forgiveness have a social aspect."

6. The USCC's *Reflections on the Sacrament* acknowledged that "there have not been many diocesan-level initiatives with regard to the Sacrament of Penance," and observed that "*most catechesis of adults has occurred through their involvement in the preparation of their children for the sacraments of initiation*" (p. 4; emphasis mine).

7. John M. Huels, *The Pastoral Companion: A Canon Law Handbook for Catholic Ministry*, 3rd ed. rev. (Quincy, IL: Franciscan Press, 2002). Pages 145–48 deal specifically with the remission of the penalty for abortion.

8. *New Commentary on the Code of Canon Law*, ed. John P. Beal, James A. Coriden, Thomas J. Green, commissioned by the Canon Law Society of America (Mahwah, NJ: Paulist Press, 2000). The commentary on the canons pertaining to the sacrament of reconciliation was written by Frederick R. McManus.

9. The two canons in their entirety are as follows: "The sacramental seal is inviolable; therefore it is absolutely forbidden for a confessor to betray in any way a penitent in words or in any manner and for any reason" (can. 983 §1); "The interpreter, if there is one, and all others who in any way have knowledge of sins from confession are also obliged to observe secrecy" (§2). "A confessor is prohibited completely from using knowledge acquired from confession to the detriment of the penitent even when any danger of revelation is excluded" (can. 984 §1); "A person who has been placed in authority cannot use in any manner for external governance the knowledge about sins which he has received in confession at any time" (§2).

10. Huels, *Pastoral Companion*, p. 134.

Chapter Three

1. USCC, *Reflections on the Sacrament of Penance*, for example, reports that parishioners "strongly supported the statement that [they] are looking for an opportunity for moral and spiritual discernment in the Sacrament of Penance" (p. 11).

2. Rahner, "Problems Concerning Confession," p. 201, emphasis mine.

Chapter Four

1. Some forty years ago the postconciliar commission charged with revising the rite of penance proposed that several different formulae of sacramental absolution be approved. In this way, it was thought, a confessor could choose the version that would address more specifically the situation of a particular penitent. The suggestion was rejected, and so we have one formula with which we address penitents of all ages and absolve all sins, be they mortal or venial. I consider this unfortunate, since the sacramental formula of any of the sacraments is the "verbal core" of the celebration, and so should reflect vividly and as personally as possible the meaning the person has approached the sacrament for. One hopes that future study and revision of the rite of reconciliation will provide several sacramental forms: one addressed to those conscious of grave sin, another to those whose sins are of the ordinary, daily variety—and, perhaps, one specifically designed for celebrating the sacrament with children.

2. *Catechism*, par. 1466.

3. Concerning the example in this section of the husband bringing to the sacrament his difficulties with the Church's teaching on birth control, I wish to call attention to the "*Vademecum* for Confessors Concerning Some Aspects of the Morality of Conjugal Life." This 1997 document, published by the Pontifical Council for the Family, is reprinted in its entirety as Appendix I of this book. It contains many guidelines and pastoral suggestions pertinent to our sacramental ministry to married couples.

4. Bernard Häring, *Shalom: Peace—The Sacrament of Reconciliation* (Garden City, NY: Doubleday & Company, Inc.: Image Books, rev. ed., 1969), pp. 69–70, emphasis in original.

5. *Vademecum*, Section 3, par. 2.

6. *Vademecum*, Section 3, par. 5.

7. *Vademecum*, Section 3, par. 11.

8. David M. Coffey, *The Sacrament of Reconciliation*, *Lex Orandi* series, ed. John D. Laurance (Collegeville: Liturgical Press, 2001), p.110, emphasis in original. See also Fr. Karl Rahner's reflection, "The Meaning of Frequent Confession of Devotion," in *Theological Investigations III*, pp. 177–89.

9. In line with this, see my reflections in Appendix III, "Confessors Need to Be Penitents, Too."

10. John Paul II, *Reconciliation and Penance*, par. 32.

11. See "Celebrating the Sacrament of Penance" (Washington, DC: USCCB, 2003). The text of this pamphlet is available from the USCCB's website (www.usccb.org) under "Publications/Liturgy and Prayer/Sacraments."

12. Coffey, *The Sacrament of Reconciliation*, p. 149. His insightful comments on Rite II are on pp. 148–53.

13. *Rite of Penance*, Introduction, no. 40, dealing with "Adaptations of the Rite to Various Regions and Circumstances," states: "It is for priests, and especially parish priests (pastors): a. in celebrating reconciliation with individuals or with a community, to adapt the rite to the concrete circumstances of the penitents. They must preserve the essential structure and the entire form of absolution, but if necessary they may omit some parts of the rite for pastoral reasons or enlarge upon them, may select the texts of readings or prayers, and may choose a place more suitable for the celebration according to the regulations of the conference of bishops, so that the entire celebration may be enriching and effective...."

14. For this insight I am indebted to the article by Paul A. Riemann, "Am I My Brother's Keeper?" in *Interpretation* (October 1970), 482–91. I thank my Old Testament professor at Saint Meinrad Seminary, Fr. Damian Dietlein, O.S.B., monk of Assumption Abbey, for calling my attention to Riemann's insights.

Concluding Remarks

1. Rahner, "Problems Concerning Confession," p. 205, emphasis mine. Also recommended in this regard is Father Rahner's "Guilt and its Remission: The Borderland between Theology and Psychotherapy" in *Theological Investigations II: Man in the Church* (Baltimore: Helicon Press, 1963), pp. 265–81.

2. John Paul II, *Reconciliation and Penance*, par. 29.

Appendix I

VADEMECUM FOR CONFESSORS CONCERNING SOME ASPECTS OF THE MORALITY OF CONJUGAL LIFE

The official English translation of the "*Vademecum* for Confessors Concerning Some Aspects of the Morality of Conjugal Life" follows. The Vatican's Pontifical Council for the Family published this "companion for confessors" in February 1997.

In its own words, the *Vademecum* "consists of a set of propositions which confessors are to keep in mind while administering the sacrament of Reconciliation, in order to better help married couples to live their vocation to fatherhood or motherhood in a Christian way, within their own personal and social circumstances."

An introduction outlines the document's intention and briefly reviews Church doctrine on conjugal chastity and the goods of marriage. The *Vademecum* proper begins with an eleven-paragraph commentary on "Holiness in Marriage" and "The Teaching of the Church on Responsible Procreation." Nineteen subsequent paragraphs—appropriately, the document's lengthiest section—offer insights and guidelines under the heading, "Pastoral Guidelines for Confessors."

I have included the *Vademecum* in my book because it is yet another—and an official—example of what I have tried

137

to offer: guidelines and principles upon which we can reflect and consider, so that we may minister the sacrament of peace more effectively and with greater confidence. I recommend a careful study of the document and its excellent, substantial footnotes.

CONTENTS

PRESENTATION

Through his Church, Christ continues the mission he received from the Father. He sent the *Twelve* to proclaim the kingdom and to call people to repentance and conversion, to *metanoia* (cf. Mk 6:12). The risen Christ transmitted his own power of reconciliation to them: "Receive the Holy Spirit. Whose sins you forgive, are forgiven them" (John 20:22–23). Through the outpouring of the Spirit effected by Christ, the Church continues the preaching of the Gospel, inviting people to conversion, and administering the sacrament of the remission of sins, by means of which repentant sinners obtain reconciliation with God and with the Church and see the way of salvation opening up before them.

This *vademecum* traces its origin to the particular pastoral sensitivity of the Holy Father, who has entrusted the task of preparing this aid for confessors to the Pontifical Council for the Family. With the experience he acquired both as a priest and a bishop, the Pope ascertained the importance of clear and certain guidelines to which the ministers of the sacrament of *Reconciliation* can refer in their dialogue with souls. The richness of the doctrine of the Magisterium of the Church on themes of marriage and the family, especially since the Second Vatican Council, has raised the need for a good synthesis regarding *some questions of morality pertaining to conjugal life.*

If, on a doctrinal level, the Church has a solid awareness of the requirements of the sacrament of Penance, it cannot be denied that a certain void has been forming with regard to implementing these teachings in pastoral practice. The doctrinal data, therefore, is the foundation supporting this *vade-*

mecum, and it is not our task to repeat it here, although it is called to mind in various passages. We know well all the richness that has been offered to the Christian community by the Encyclical *Humanae Vitae* illuminated then by the Encyclical *Veritatis Splendor* and by the Apostolic Exhortations, *Familiaris Consortio* and *Reconciliatio et Paenitentia*. We also know how the *Catechism of the Catholic Church* has provided an effective and synthetic summary of the Church's doctrine on these subjects.

"To evoke conversion and penance in man's heart and to offer him the gift of reconciliation is the specific mission of the Church....It is not a mission which consists merely of a few theoretical statements and the presentation of an ethical ideal unaccompanied by the energy with which to carry it out. Rather it seeks to express itself in precise ministerial functions directed toward a concrete practice of penance and reconciliation" *(Apostolic Exhortation Reconciliatio et Paenitentia, 23)*.

We are happy to put this document in the hands of priests, a document that has been prepared at the request of the Holy Father with the aid of the competent collaboration of professors of theology as well as some pastors. We thank all those who have offered their contribution to making this document possible. We are especially grateful to the Congregation for the Doctrine of the Faith and the Apostolic Penitentiary.

INTRODUCTION

1. Aim of the Document

The family, which the Second Vatican Council has defined as the *domestic sanctuary of the Church*, and as "the primary vital cell of society,"[1] constitutes a privileged object of the Church's pastoral attention. "At a moment of history in which the family is the object of numerous forces that seek to destroy it or in some way to deform it, and aware that the well-being of society and her own good are intimately tied to the good of the family, the Church perceives in a more urgent and compelling way her mission of proclaiming to all people the plan of God for marriage and the family."[2]

Over recent years, the Church, through the words of the Holy Father and a vast spiritual mobilization of pastors and lay people, has greatly increased her concern to help the entire community of the faithful to consider with gratitude and fullness of faith, the gifts given by God to men and women united in the sacrament of Marriage, so that they may be able to realize an authentic path of holiness and offer a truly evangelical witness in the concrete situations of life in which they find themselves.

The sacrament of the Eucharist and the sacrament of Penance play a fundamental role in this path toward marital and domestic holiness. The former reinforces union with Christ, the source of grace and life, and the latter rebuilds it, whenever it has been destroyed, or increases and perfects conjugal and family unity,[3] menaced and wounded by sin.

To help married couples be aware of the path of their holiness and to carry out their mission, it is fundamental that their conscience be formed, and that God's will be fulfilled in the specific area of married life, that is, in their conjugal communion and service for life. The light of the Gospel and the grace of the sacrament represent the indispensable elements for the elevation and the fullness of conjugal love that has its source in God the Creator. In fact, "the Lord, wishing to bestow special gifts of grace and divine love on it, has restored, perfected and elevated it."[4]

The moment in which the spouses ask for and receive the sacrament of Reconciliation represents a salvific event of the greatest importance for accepting the demands of authentic love and of God's plan in their daily life. It provides an illuminating occasion for deepening their faith and a concrete aid in carrying out God's plan in their lives.

"It is the sacrament of Penance or Reconciliation that prepares the way for each individual, even those weighed down with great faults. In this sacrament each person can experience mercy in a unique way, that is, the love which is more powerful than sin."[5]

Since the administration of the sacrament of Reconciliation is entrusted to the ministry of priests, this document is addressed specifically to confessors and seeks to offer some practical guidelines for the confession and absolution of the faithful in matters of conjugal chastity. More specifically, this *vademecum ad praxim confessariorum* intends also to offer a reference point for married penitents so that they can draw ever greater advantage from the practice of the sacrament of Reconciliation, and live their vocation to responsible parenthood in keeping with divine law, authoritatively taught by the Church. It will also serve as an aid for those who are preparing for marriage.

The problem of responsible procreation represents a particularly delicate point in Catholic moral teaching relating to conjugal life. This is especially the case with regard to the administration of the sacrament of Reconciliation, in which doctrinal affirmations confront concrete human situations and the spiritual paths of the individual faithful. It has become necessary, in fact, to recall firm points of reference which make it possible to deal pastorally both with new methods of contraception and the aggravation of the entire phenomenon.[6] This document does not intend to repeat the entire teaching of the Encyclical *Humanae Vitae*, the Apostolic Exhortation *Familiaris Consortio*, and other documents of the ordinary Magisterium of the Supreme Pontiff, but only to offer suggestions and guidelines for the spiritual good of the faithful who have recourse to the sacrament of Reconciliation, and to overcome possible discrepancies and uncertainties in the practice of confessors.

2. Conjugal Chastity in the Doctrine of the Church

Christian tradition has always upheld the goodness and honesty of the marital union and of the family against numerous heresies which arose from the very beginnings of the Church. Willed by God with creation itself, brought back to its primal origin and elevated to the dignity of a sacrament by Christ, marriage consists of an intimate communion of the spouses of love and life, intrinsically ordered to the good of the children that God wishes to entrust to them. Both for the good of the spouses and of the children, as well as for the good of society itself, the natural bond no longer depends on human decision.[7]

The virtue of conjugal chastity "involves the integrity of the person and the integrality of the gift,"[8] and through it sexuality "becomes personal and truly human when it is integrated into the relationship of one person to another, in the complete and lifelong mutual gift of a man and a woman."[9]

This virtue, insofar as it refers to the intimate relations of the spouses, requires that "the total meaning of mutual self-giving and human procreation in the context of true love"[10] be maintained. Therefore, among the fundamental moral principles of conjugal life, it is necessary to keep in mind "the inseparable connection, willed by God and unable to be broken by man on his own initiative, between the two meanings of the conjugal act: the unitive meaning and the procreative meaning."[11]

Throughout this century the Supreme Pontiffs have issued various documents expounding the principal moral truths on conjugal chastity. Among these, special mention is due to the Encyclical *Casti Connubii* (1930) of Pius XI,[12] numerous discourses of Pius Xll,[13] the Encyclical *Humanae Vitae* (1968) of Paul VI,[14] the Apostolic Exhortation *Familiaris Consortio*[15] (1981), the Letter to Families *Gratissimam Sane*[16] and the Encyclical *Evangelium Vitae* (1995) of John Paul II. Together with these, the Pastoral Constitution *Gaudium et Spes*[17] (1965) and the *Catechism of the Catholic Church*[18] (1992) deserve special mention. Important also, in keeping with these teachings, are some documents of the episcopal conferences, as well as those of pastors and theologians who have developed the subject and given it a deeper understanding. The example should also be mentioned of many married persons, whose commitment to live human love in a Christian way constitutes a most effective contribution for the new evangelization of the family.

3. The "Goods" of Marriage and the Gift of Self

By means of the sacrament of Marriage, married couples receive from Christ the Redeemer the gift of grace that confirms and elevates the communion of faithful and fruitful love. The holiness to which they are called is above all a *grace given.*

The persons called to live in the married state realize their vocation to love[19] in the full gift of self which adequately expresses the language of the body.[20] From the mutual gift of the spouses comes, as its fruit, the gift of life to the children, who are a sign and crowning of their spousal love.[21]

Contraception, directly opposed to the transmission of life, betrays and falsifies the self-sacrificing love proper to marriage, "altering its value of total self-giving"[22] and contradicting God's design of love in which it has been granted to married couples to participate.

Vademecum for the Use of Confessors

This *vademecum* consists of a set of propositions which confessors are to keep in mind while administering the sacrament of Reconciliation, in order to better help married couples to live their vocation to fatherhood or motherhood in a Christian way, within their own personal and social circumstances.

1. Holiness in Marriage

1. All Christians must be fittingly made aware of their call to holiness. The invitation to follow Christ addressed, in fact, to each and every member of the faithful, must tend toward the fullness of the Christian life and to the perfection of charity in each one's own state.[23]

2. Charity is the soul of holiness. By its very nature, charity—a gift that the Spirit infuses in the heart—assumes and elevates human love and makes it capable of the perfect gift of self. Charity makes renunciation more acceptable, lightens the spiritual struggle and renders more joyous the gift of self.[24]

3. Human beings cannot achieve perfect self-giving with their own forces alone. They become capable of this by the grace of the Holy Spirit. In effect it is Christ who reveals the original truth of marriage, and, freeing man from all hardness of heart, renders him capable of fully realizing it.[25]

4. On the path to holiness, a Christian experiences both human weakness and the benevolence and mercy of the Lord. Therefore, the keystone of the exercise of Christian virtues—

and thus also of conjugal chastity—rests on faith which makes us aware of God's mercy, and on repentance which humbly receives divine forgiveness.[26]

5. The spouses carry out the full gift of self in married life and in conjugal union which, for Christians, is vivified by the grace of the sacrament. Their specific union and the transmission of life are tasks proper to their conjugal holiness.[27]

2. The Teaching of the Church on Responsible Procreation

1. The spouses are to be strengthened in their view of the inestimable value and preciousness of human life, and aided so that they may commit themselves to making their own family a sanctuary of life:[28] *"God himself is present in human fatherhood and motherhood* quite differently than he is present in all other instances of begetting 'on earth.'"[29]

2. Parents are to consider their mission as an honor and a responsibility, since they become cooperators with the Lord in calling into existence a new human person, made in the image and likeness of God, redeemed and destined, in Christ, to a life of eternal happiness.[30] "It is precisely in their role as coworkers with God *who transmits his image to the new creature* that we see the greatness of couples who are ready 'to cooperate with the love of the Creator and the Savior, who through them will enlarge and enrich his own family day by day.'"[31]

3. From this the Christian's joy and esteem for paternity and maternity are derived. This parenthood is called *"responsible"* in recent documents of the Church, to emphasize the awareness and generosity of the spouses with regard to their mission of transmitting life, which has in itself a value of eternity, and to call attention to their role as educators. Certainly it is a duty of married couples—who, for that matter, should

seek appropriate counsel—to deliberate deeply and in a spirit of faith about the size of their family, and to decide the concrete mode of realizing it, with respect for the moral criteria of conjugal life.[32]

4. The Church has always taught the intrinsic evil of contraception, that is, of every marital act intentionally rendered unfruitful. This teaching is to be held as definitive and irreformable. Contraception is gravely opposed to marital chastity; it is contrary to the good of the transmission of life (the procreative aspect of matrimony), and to the reciprocal self-giving of the spouses (the unitive aspect of matrimony); it harms true love and denies the sovereign role of God in the transmission of human life.[33]

5. A specific and more serious moral evil is present in the use of means which have an abortive effect, impeding the implantation of the embryo which has just been fertilized or even causing its expulsion in an early stage of pregnancy.[34]

6. However, profoundly different from any contraceptive practice is the behavior of married couples, who, always remaining fundamentally open to the gift of life, live their intimacy only in the unfruitful periods, when they are led to this course by serious motives of responsible parenthood. This is true both from the anthropological and moral points of view, because it is rooted in a different conception of the person and of sexuality.[35]

The witness of couples who for years have lived in harmony with the plan of the Creator, and who, for proportionately serious reasons, licitly use the methods rightly called "natural," confirms that it is possible for spouses to live the demands of chastity and of married life with common accord and full self-giving.

3. Pastoral Guidelines for Confessors

1. In dealing with penitents on the matter of responsible procreation, the confessor should keep four aspects in mind: a) the example of the Lord who "is capable of reaching down to every prodigal son, to every human misery, and above all to every form of moral misery, to sin";[36] b) a prudent reserve in inquiring into these sins; c) help and encouragement to the penitents so that they may be able to reach sufficient repentance and accuse themselves fully of grave sins; d) advice which inspires all, in a gradual way, to embrace the path of holiness.

2. The minister of Reconciliation should always keep in mind that the sacrament has been instituted for men and women who are sinners. Therefore barring manifest proof to the contrary, he will receive the penitents who approach the confessional taking for granted their good will to be reconciled with the merciful God, a good will that is born, although in different degrees, of *a contrite and humbled heart* (Ps 51:19).[37]

3. When occasional penitents approach the sacrament, those who have not confessed for a long time and manifest a grave general situation, it is necessary, before asking direct and concrete questions with regard to responsible procreation and chastity in general, to enlighten them so that they can understand these duties in a vision of faith. Thus it will be necessary, if the accusation of sins has been too succinct or mechanical, to help the penitents to place their life before God, and, with general questions on various virtues and/or obligations in accordance with their personal conditions,[38] remind them in a positive way of the invitation to the sanctity of love and of the importance of their duties in the area of procreation and the education of children.

4. When it is the penitent who asks questions or seeks clarification on specific points, even if only implicitly, the confes-

sor will have to respond adequately, but always with prudence and discretion,[39] without approving erroneous opinions.

5. The confessor is bound to admonish penitents regarding objectively grave transgressions of God's law and to ensure that they truly desire absolution and God's pardon with the resolution to re-examine and correct their behavior. Frequent relapse into sins of contraception does not in itself constitute a motive for denying absolution; absolution cannot be imparted, however, in the absence of sufficient repentance or of the resolution not to fall again into sin.[40]

6. The penitent who regularly confesses with the same priest frequently seeks something besides absolution alone. The confessor needs to know how to provide guidance to help him or her to improve in all Christian virtues, and, in consequence, in the sanctification of marital life.[41] This certainly will be easier where a relationship of actual spiritual direction exists, even if this name is not used.

7. On the part of the penitent, the sacrament of Reconciliation requires sincere sorrow, a formally complete accusation of mortal sins, and the resolution, with the help of God, not to fall into sin again. In general, it is not necessary for the confessor to investigate concerning sins committed in invincible ignorance of their evil, or due to an inculpable error of judgment. Although these sins are not imputable, they do not cease, however, to be an evil and a disorder. This also holds for *the objective evil of contraception*, which introduces a pernicious habit into the conjugal life of the couple. It is therefore necessary to strive in the most suitable way to free the moral conscience from those errors[42] which contradict the nature of conjugal life as a total gift.

Though one must keep in mind that the formation of consciences is to be accomplished above all in catechesis for married couples, both general or specific, it is always necessary to assist the spouses, also in the moment of the sacrament of Reconciliation, to examine themselves on the specific duties of conjugal life. Whenever the confessor considers it necessary to question the penitent, he should do so with discretion and respect.

8. The principle according to which it is preferable to let penitents remain in good faith in cases of error due to subjectively invincible ignorance, is certainly to be considered always valid, even in matters of conjugal chastity. And this applies whenever it is foreseen that the penitent, although oriented toward living within the bounds of a life of faith, would not be prepared to change his own conduct but rather would begin formally to sin. Nonetheless in these cases, the confessor must try to bring such penitents ever closer to accepting God's plan in their own lives, even in these demands, by means of prayer, admonition and exhorting them to form their consciences, and by the teaching of the Church.

9. The pastoral "law of gradualness," not to be confused with the "gradualness of the law" which would tend to diminish the demands it places on us, consists of requiring a *decisive break* with sin together with a *progressive path* toward total union with the will of God and with his loving demands.[43]

10. On the other hand, to presume to make one's own weakness the criterion of moral truth is unacceptable. From the very first proclamation of the word of Jesus, Christians realize that there is a "disproportion" between the moral law, natural and evangelical, and the human capacity. They equally understand that the recognition of their own weakness is the necessary and secure road by which the doors to God's mercy will be opened.[44]

11. Sacramental absolution is not to be denied to those who, repentant after having gravely sinned against conjugal

chastity, demonstrate the desire to strive to abstain from sinning again, notwithstanding relapses. In accordance with the approved doctrine and practice followed by the holy doctors and confessors with regard to habitual penitents, the confessor is to avoid demonstrating lack of trust either in the grace of God or in the dispositions of the penitent, by exacting humanly impossible absolute guarantees of an irreproachable future conduct.[45]

12. When the penitent shows a willingness to accept the moral teaching, especially in the case of one who habitually frequents the sacrament and demonstrates trust with regard to the spiritual help it offers, it is good to instill confidence in divine Providence and be supportive, in order to help the penitent to examine himself honestly before God. For this purpose it will be necessary to verify the solidity of the motives inducing a limitation of fatherhood or motherhood, and the liceity of the methods chosen to distance or avoid a new birth.

13. Special difficulties are presented by cases of cooperation in the sin of a spouse who voluntarily renders the unitive act infecund. In the first place, it is necessary to distinguish cooperation in the proper sense, from violence or unjust imposition on the part of one of the spouses, which the other spouse in fact cannot resist.[46] This cooperation can be licit when the three following conditions are jointly met:

1) when the action of the cooperating spouse is not already illicit in itself;[47]
2) when proportionally grave reasons exist for cooperating in the sin of the other spouse;
3) when one is seeking to help the other spouse to desist from such conduct (patiently, with prayer, charity and dialogue; although not necessarily in that moment, nor on every single occasion).

14. Furthermore, it is necessary to carefully evaluate the question of cooperation in evil when recourse is made to means which can have an abortifacient effect.[48]

15. Christian couples are witnesses of God's love in the world. They must therefore be convinced, with the assistance of faith and even in spite of their experience of human weakness, that it is possible to observe the will of the Lord in conjugal life with divine grace. Frequent and persevering recourse to prayer, to the Eucharist and to the sacrament of Reconciliation, are indispensable for gaining mastery of self.[49]

16. Priests, in their catechesis and in their preparation of couples for marriage, are asked to maintain uniform criteria with regard to the evil of the contraceptive act, both in their teaching and in the area of the sacrament of Reconciliation, in complete fidelity to the Magisterium of the Church.

Bishops are to take particular care to be vigilant in this regard, for not infrequently the faithful are scandalized by this lack of unity, both in the area of catechesis as well as in the sacrament of Reconciliation.[50]

17. The pastoral practice of confession will be more effective if it is united to an ongoing and thorough catechesis on the Christian vocation to marital love and on its joyful and demanding dimensions, its grace and personal commitment,[51] and if consultors and centers are made available to which confessors could easily refer penitents in order to acquire adequate knowledge about the natural methods.

18. In order to render the moral directives concerning responsible procreation concretely applicable, it is necessary that the precious work of confessors be completed by catechesis.[52] Accurate illumination of consciences with regard to the sin of abortion certainly forms an integral part of this task.

19. Regarding absolution for the sin of abortion, the obligation always exists to have regard for the canonical norms. If

repentance is sincere and it is difficult to send the penitent to the competent authority to whom the absolution of the censure is reserved, every confessor can absolve according to canon 1357, suggesting an adequate penitential act, and indicating the necessity to have recourse, possibly offering to draft and forward it himself.[53]

Especially in these times, the Church considers it to be one of her principal duties to proclaim the mystery of mercy, revealed in a supreme degree in the Person of Jesus Christ, and to bring mercy into life.[54]

The pre-eminent setting for proclaiming and realizing mercy is the celebration of the sacrament of Reconciliation.

Precisely this first year of the triennium of preparation for the Third Millennium, dedicated to *Christ Jesus, the only Savior of the world, yesterday, today and for ever* (cf. Heb 13:8), can offer a great opportunity for the work of pastoral renewal and catechetical deepening in the dioceses, and specifically in shrines visited by many pilgrims where the sacrament of forgiveness is administered with an abundant availability of confessors.

May priests always be fully available for this ministry on which the eternal beatitude of married couples depends, and also upon which, in good part, their serenity and happiness in this present life rests. May priests truly be for them living witnesses of the Father's mercy!

Vatican City, February 12, 1997

Alfonso Cardinal Lopez Trujillo
President of the Pontifical Council for the Family
Francisco Gil Hellin
Secretary

NOTES TO *Vademecum*

1. Vatican Council II, Decree on the Apostolate of the Laity *Apostolicam Actuositatem* (November 18, 1965), 11.

2. John Paul II, Apostolic Exhortation *Familiaris Consortio* (November 22, 1981), 3.

3. Cf. John Paul II, Apostolic Exhortation *Familiaris Consortio* (November 22, 1981), 58.

4. Second Vatican Ecumenical Council, Pastoral Constitution on the Church in the Modern World *Gaudium et Spes* (December 7, 1965), 49.

5. John Paul II, Encyclical *Dives in Misericordia* (November 30, 1980), 13.

6. The abortifacient effect of new pharmaceutical products must be borne in mind. Cf. John Paul II, Encyclical *Evangelium Vitae* (March 25, 1995), 13.

7. Cf. Second Vatican Ecumenical Council, Pastoral Constitution on the Church in the Modern World *Gaudium et Spes* (December 7, 1965), 48.

8. *Catechism of the Catholic Church* (October 11, 1992), 2337.

9. *Ibid.*

10. Second Vatican Ecumenical Council, Pastoral Constitution on the Church in the Modern World *Gaudium et Spes* (December 7, 1965), 51.

11. Paul VI, Encyclical *Humanae Vitae* (July 25, 1968), 12.

12. Pius XI, Encyclical *Casti Connubii* (December 31, 1930).

13. Pius XII, *Allocution to the Congress of the Catholic Union of Italian Midwives* (October 2, 1951), *Discourse to the Union of the Family (Fronte della famiglia) and to the Associations of Numerous Families* (November 27, 1951).

14. Paul VI, Encyclical *Humanae Vitae* (July 25, 1968).

15. John Paul II, Apostolic Exhortation *Familiaris Consortio* (November 22, 1981).

16. John Paul II, Letter to Families *Gratissimam Sane* (February 2, 1994).

17. Second Vatican Ecumenical Council, Pastoral Constitution on the Church in the Modern World *Gaudium et Spes* (December 7, 1965).

18. *Catechism of the Catholic Church* (October 11, 1992).

19. Cf. Second Vatican Ecumenical Council, Pastoral Constitution on the Church in the Modern World *Gaudium et Spes* (December 7, 1965), 24.

20. John Paul II, Apostolic Exhortation *Familiaris Consortio* (November 22, 1981), 32.

21. Cf. *Catechism of the Catholic Church*, 2378, cf. John Paul II, Letter to Families *Gratissimam Sane* (February 2, 1994), 11.

22. John Paul II, Apostolic Exhortation *Familiaris Consortio* (November 22, 1981), 32.

23. "The forms and tasks of life are many but holiness is one—that sanctity which is cultivated by all who act under God's Spirit and, obeying the Father's voice and adoring God the Father in spirit and in truth, follow Christ poor, humble and cross-bearing, that they may deserve to be partakers of his glory. Each one, however, according to his own gifts and duties must steadfastly advance along the way of a living faith, which arouses hope and works through love" (Second Vatican Ecumenical Council, Dogmatic Constitution on the Church *Lumen Gentium*, November 21, 1964, 41).

24. "Charity is the soul of the holiness to which all are called" (*Catechism of the Catholic Church*, 826). "Love causes man to find fulfillment through the sincere gift of self. To love means to give and to receive something which can be neither bought nor sold, but only given freely and mutually" (John Paul II, Letter to Families *Gratissimam Sane*, February 2, 1994, 11).

25. Cf. John Paul II, Apostolic Exhortation *Familiaris Consortio* (November 22, 1981), 13.

"Keeping God's law in particular situations can be difficult, extremely difficult, but it is never impossible. This is the constant teaching of the Church's tradition" (John Paul II, Encyclical *Veritatis Splendor*, August 6, 1993, 102).

"It would be a very grave error to conclude that the norm taught by the Church is in itself only an 'ideal' which must then be adapted, put in proportion, aligned, they say, with the concrete possibilities of man, according to a 'weighing of the various goods in question.' But what are the 'concrete possibilities of man'? And of *what* man are we speaking? Of man *dominated* by concupiscence or of man *redeemed by Christ*? For this is the matter under consideration: the *reality* of the redemption of Christ. *Christ has redeemed us!* This means: he has given us the *possibility* of realizing the *entire* truth of our being. He has liberated our liberty from the *domination* of concupiscence. And if redeemed man sins again, that is not due to the imperfection of the redeeming act of Christ, but to the *will* of man who subtracts himself from the grace gushing out from that act. The commandment of God is certainly proportioned to the capacities of man, but to the capacities of man to whom the Holy Spirit has been given, the man who, if he has fallen into sin, can always obtain pardon and enjoy the presence of the Spirit" (John Paul II, *Discourse to Participants in a Course on Responsible Procreation*, March 1, 1984).

26. "*To acknowledge one's sin*, indeed—penetrating still more deeply into the consideration of one's own personhood—to recognize oneself as being a sinner, capable of sin and inclined to commit sin, is the essential first step in returning to God....In effect, to become reconciled with God presupposes and includes detaching oneself consciously and with determination from the sin into which one has fallen. It presupposes and includes, therefore, doing penance in the fullest sense of the term: repenting, showing this repentance, adopting a real attitude of repentance—which is the attitude of the person who starts out on the road of return to the Father....In the concrete circumstances of sinful humanity, in which there can be no conversion without the acknowledgment of one's own sin, the Church's ministry intervenes in each individual case with a precise penitential purpose. That is, the Church's ministry intervenes in order to bring the person to the 'knowledge of self'"

(John Paul II, Post-Synodal Apostolic Exhortation *Reconciliatio et Paenitentia*, December 2, 1984, 13).

"When we realize that God's love for us does not cease in the face of our sin or recoil before our offenses, but becomes even more attentive and generous; when we realize that this love went so far as to cause the passion and death of the Word made flesh who consented to redeem us at the price of his own blood, then we exclaim in gratitude: 'Yes, the Lord is rich in mercy,' and even: 'The Lord *is* mercy'" (*ibid.*, 22).

27. "Christian spouses and parents are included in the universal call to sanctity. For them this call is specified by the sacrament they have celebrated and is carried out concretely in the realities proper to their conjugal and family life. This gives rise to the grace and requirement of an authentic and profound *conjugal and family spirituality* that draws its inspiration from the themes of creation, covenant, cross, resurrection and sign" (John Paul II, Apostolic Exhortation *Familiaris Consortio*, November 22, 1981, 56).

"Authentic married love is caught up into divine love and is directed and enriched by the redemptive power of Christ and the salvific action of the Church, with the result that the spouses are effectively led to God and are helped and strengthened in their lofty role as fathers and mothers. Spouses, therefore, are fortified and, as it were, consecrated for the duties and dignity of their state by a special sacrament; fulfilling their conjugal and family role by virtue of this sacrament, spouses are penetrated with the spirit of Christ and their whole life is suffused by faith, hope, and charity; thus they increasingly further their own perfection and their mutual sanctification, and together they render glory to God" (Second Vatican Ecumenical Council, Pastoral Constitution on the Church in the Modern World *Gaudium et Spes*, December 7, 1965, 48).

28. "But the Church firmly believes that human life, even if weak and suffering, is always a splendid gift of God's goodness. Against the pessimism and selfishness which cast a shadow over the world, the Church stands for life. In each human life she sees the *Splendor* of that 'Yes,' that 'Amen,' who is Christ himself. To the 'no' which assails and afflicts the world, she replies with this living

'Yes', thus defending the human person and the world from all who plot against and harm life" (John Paul II, Apostolic Exhortation *Familiaris Consortio*, November 22, 1981, 30).

"It is necessary to go back to seeing the family as the *sanctuary of life*. The family is indeed sacred: it is the place in which life—the gift of God—can be properly welcomed and protected against the many attacks to which it is exposed, and can develop in accordance with what constitutes authentic human growth. In the face of the so-called culture of death, the family is the heart of the culture of life" (John Paul II, Encyclical *Centesimus Annus*, May 1, 1991, 39).

29. John Paul II, Letter to Families *Gratissimam Sane* (February 2, 1994), 9.

30. "God himself said: 'It is not good that man should be alone' (Gen 2:18) and 'from the beginning [he] made them male and female' (Matt 19:4); wishing to associate them in a special way with his own creative work, God blessed man and woman with the words: 'Be fruitful and multiply' (Gen 1:28). Without intending to underestimate the other ends of marriage, it must be said that true married love and the whole structure of family life which results from it is directed to disposing the spouses to cooperate valiantly with the love of the Creator and Savior who through them will increase and enrich his family from day to day" (Second Vatican Ecumenical Council, Pastoral Constitution on the Church in the Modern World *Gaudium et Spes*, December 7, 1965, 50).

"The Christian family is a communion of persons, a sign and image of the communion of the Father and the Son in the Holy Spirit. In the procreation and education of children it reflects the Father's work of creation" (*Catechism of the Catholic Church*, 2205).

"Cooperating with God to call new human beings into existence means contributing to the transmission of that divine image and likeness of which everyone 'born of a woman' is a bearer" (John Paul II, Letter to Families *Gratissimam Sane*, February 2, 1994, 8).

31. John Paul II, Encyclical *Evangelium Vitae* (March 25, 1995), 43; cf. Second Vatican Ecumenical Council, Pastoral

Constitution on the Church in the Modern World *Gaudium et Spes* (December 7, 1965), 50.

32. "Married couples should regard it as their proper mission to transmit human life and to educate their children; they should realize that they are thereby cooperating with the love of God the Creator and are, in a certain sense, its interpreters. This involves the fulfillment of their role with a sense of human and Christian responsibility and the formation of correct judgments through docile respect for God and common reflection and effort; it also involves a consideration of their own good and the good of their children already born or yet to come, an ability to read the signs of the times and of their own situation on the material and spiritual level, and, finally, an estimation of the good of the family, of society, and of the Church. It is the married couple themselves who must in the last analysis arrive at these judgments before God. Married people should realize that in their behavior they may not simply follow their own fancy but must be ruled by conscience—and conscience ought to be conformed to the law of God in the light of the teaching authority of the Church, which is the authentic interpreter of divine law. For the divine law throws light on the meaning of married love, protects it and leads it to truly human fulfillment" (Second Vatican Ecumenical Council, Pastoral Constitution on the Church in the Modern World *Gaudium et Spes*, December 7, 1965, 50).

"When it is a question of harmonizing married love with the responsible transmission of life, it is not enough to take only the good intention and the evaluation of motives into account; the objective criteria must be used, criteria drawn from the nature of the human person and the human action, criteria which respect the total meaning of mutual self-giving and human procreation in the context of true love; all this is possible only if the virtue of married chastity is seriously practiced. In questions of birth regulation the sons of the Church, faithful to these principles, are forbidden to use methods disapproved of by the teaching authority of the Church" (Second Vatican Ecumenical Council, Pastoral Constitution on the Church in the Modern World *Gaudium et Spes*, December 7, 1965, 51).

Appendix I: Notes to Vademecum

"In relation to physical, economic, psychological and social conditions, responsible parenthood is exercised, either by the deliberate and generous decision to raise a numerous family, or by the decision, made for grave motives and with due respect for the moral law, to avoid for the time being, or even for an indeterminate period, a new birth.

"Responsible parenthood also and above all implies a more profound relationship to the objective moral order established by God, of which a right conscience is the faithful interpreter. The responsible exercise of parenthood implies, therefore, that husband and wife recognize fully their own duties toward God, toward themselves, toward the family and toward society, in a correct hierarchy of values.

"In the task of transmitting life, therefore, they are not free to proceed completely at will, as if they could determine in a wholly autonomous way the honest path to follow, but they must conform their activity to the creative intention of God, expressed in the very nature of marriage and of its acts, and manifested by the constant teaching of the Church" (Paul VI, Encyclical *Humanae Vitae*, July 25, 1968, 10).

33. The Encyclical *Humanae Vitae* declares as illicit "every action which, either in anticipation of the conjugal act, or in its accomplishment, or in the development of its natural consequences, proposes, whether as an end or as a means, to render procreation impossible." And it adds: "To justify conjugal acts made intentionally infecund, one cannot invoke as valid reasons the lesser evil, or the fact that such acts would constitute a whole together with the fecund acts already performed or to follow later, and hence would share in one and the same moral goodness. In truth if it is sometimes licit to tolerate a lesser evil in order to avoid a greater evil or to promote a greater good, it is not licit, even for the gravest reasons, to do evil so that good may follow therefrom, that is, to make into the object of a positive act of the will something which is intrinsically disorder, and hence unworthy of the human person, even when the intention is to safeguard or promote individual, family or social well-being. Consequently, it is an error to think that a conjugal act which is deliberately made infecund and so is intrinsi-

cally dishonest could be made honest and right by the ensemble of a fecund conjugal life" (Paul VI, Encyclical *Humanae Vitae*, July 25, 1968, 14).

"When couples, by means of recourse to contraception, separate these two meanings that God the Creator has inscribed in the being of man and woman and in the dynamism of their sexual communion, they act as 'arbiters' of the divine plan and they 'manipulate' and degrade human sexuality—and with it themselves and their married partner by altering its value of 'total' self-giving. Thus the innate language that expresses the total reciprocal self-giving of husband and wife is overlaid, through contraception, by an objectively contradictory language, namely, that of not giving oneself totally to the other. This leads not only to a positive refusal to be open to life, but also to a falsification of the inner truth of conjugal love, which is called upon to give itself in personal totality" (John Paul II, Apostolic Exhortation *Familiaris Consortio*, November 22, 1981, 32).

34. "The human being must be respected and treated as a person from his conception. Therefore, from that very moment the rights of a person must be accorded to him, foremost among which is the inviolable right to life of every innocent human being" (Congregation for the Doctrine of the Faith, Instruction on Respect for Human Life in Its Origin and on the Dignity of Procreation *Donum Vitae*, February 22, 1987, 1).

"Ever more clearly there emerges the strict connection which, at the level of mentality, exists between the practice of contraception and that of abortion. This is demonstrated in an alarming way also by the development of chemical preparations, intrauterine devices and injections which, distributed with the same ease as contraceptives, in reality act as abortifacients in the initial stages of development of the new human being" (John Paul II, Encyclical *Evangelium Vitae*, March 25, 1995, 13).

35. "If, then, there are serious motives to space out births, which derive from the physical or psychological conditions of husband and wife or from external conditions, the Church teaches that it is then licit to take into account the natural rhythms immanent in the generative functions, for the use of marriage in the infecund

periods only, and in this way to regulate birth without offending the moral principles which have been recalled earlier.

"The Church is coherent with herself when she considers recourse to the infecund periods to be licit, while at the same time condemning, as being always illicit, the use of means directly contrary to fecundation, even if such use is inspired by reasons which may appear honest and serious. In reality, there are essential differences between the two cases; in the former, the married couple make legitimate use of a natural disposition; in the latter, they impede the development of natural processes. It is true that, in the one and the other case, the married couple are concordant in the positive will of avoiding children for plausible reasons, seeking the certainty that offspring will not arrive, but it is also true that only in the former case are they able to renounce the use of marriage in the fecund periods when, for just motives, procreation is not desirable, while making use of it during infecund periods to manifest their affection and to safeguard their mutual fidelity. By so doing, they give proof of a truly and integrally honest love" (Paul VI, Encyclical *Humanae Vitae*, July 25, 1968, 16).

"When, instead, by means of recourse to periods of infertility, the couple respect the inseparable connection between the unitive and procreative meanings of human sexuality, they are acting as 'ministers' of God's plan and they 'benefit from' their sexuality according to the original dynamism of 'total' self-giving, without manipulation or alteration" (John Paul II, Apostolic Exhortation *Familiaris Consortio*, November 22, 1981, 32).

"The work of educating in the service of life involves the *training of married couples in responsible procreation*. In its true meaning, responsible procreation requires couples to be obedient to the Lord's call and to act as faithful interpreters of his plan. This happens when the family is generously open to new lives, and when couples maintain an attitude of openness and service to life, even if, for serious reasons and in respect for the moral law, they choose to avoid a new birth for the time being or indefinitely. The moral law obliges them in every case to control the impulse of instinct and passion, and to respect the biological laws inscribed in their person.

165

It is precisely this respect which makes legitimate, at the service of responsible procreation, the *use of natural methods of regulating fertility*" (John Paul II, Encyclical *Evangelium Vitae*, March 25, 1995, 97).

36. John Paul II, Encyclical *Dives in Misericordia* (November 30, 1980), 6.

37. "Just as at the altar where he celebrates the Eucharist and just as in each one of the sacraments, so the priest, as the minister of Penance, acts '*in persona Christi.*' The Christ whom he makes present and who accomplishes the mystery of the forgiveness of sins is the Christ who appears as the brother of man, the merciful high priest, faithful and compassionate, the shepherd intent on finding the lost sheep, the physician who heals and comforts, the one master who teaches the truth and reveals the ways of God, the judge of the living and the dead, who judges according to the truth and not according to appearances" (John Paul II, Post-Synodal Apostolic Exhortation *Reconciliatio et Paenitentia*, December 2, 1984, 29).

"When he celebrates the sacrament of Penance, the priest is fulfilling the ministry of the Good Shepherd who seeks the lost sheep, of the Good Samaritan who binds up wounds, of the Father who awaits the prodigal son and welcomes him on his return, and of the just and impartial judge whose judgment is both just and merciful. The priest is the sign and the instrument of God's merciful love for the sinner" (*Catechism of the Catholic Church*, 1465).

38. Cf. Congregation of the Holy Office *Normae quaedam de agendi ratione confessariorum circa sextum Decalogi praeceptum* (May 16, 1943).

39. "The priest in posing questions is to proceed with prudence and discretion with attention to the condition and age of the penitent, and he is to refrain from asking the name of an accomplice" (*Code of Canon Law*, can. 979).

"Accordingly, the concrete pedagogy of the Church must always remain linked with her doctrine and never be separated from it. With the same conviction as my predecessor, I therefore repeat: 'To diminish in no way the saving teaching of Christ constitutes an eminent form of charity for souls'" (John Paul II, Apostolic Exhortation *Familiaris Consortio*, November 22, 1981, 33).

40. Cf. Denzinger-Schönmetzer, *Enchiridion Symbolorum*, 3187.

41. "Confession to a priest is an essential part of the sacrament of Penance: 'All mortal sins of which penitents after a diligent self-examination are conscious must be recounted by them in confession, even if they are most secret and have been committed against the last two precepts of the Decalogue; for these sins sometimes wound the soul more grievously and are more dangerous than those which are committed openly'" (*Catechism of the Catholic Church*, 1456).

42. "If—on the contrary—the ignorance is invincible, or the moral subject is not responsible for his erroneous judgment, the evil committed by the person cannot be imputed to him. It remains no less an evil, a privation, a disorder. One must therefore work to correct the errors of moral conscience" (*Catechism of the Catholic Church*, 1793).

"It is possible that the evil done as a result of invincible ignorance or a nonculpable error of judgment may not be imputable to the agent; but even in this case it does not cease to be an evil, a disorder in relation to the truth about the good" (John Paul II, Encyclical *Veritatis Splendor*, August 6, 1993, 63).

43. "Married people too are called upon to progress unceasingly in their moral life with the support of a sincere and active desire to gain ever better knowledge of the values enshrined in and fostered by the law of God. They must also be supported by an upright and generous willingness to embody these values in their concrete decisions. They cannot, however, look on the law as merely an ideal to be achieved in the future: they must consider it as a command of Christ the Lord to overcome difficulties with constancy. 'And so what is known as "the law of gradualness" or step-by-step advance cannot be identified with "gradualness of the law" as if there were different degrees or forms of precept in God's law for different individuals and situations. In God's plan, all husbands and wives are called in marriage to holiness, and this lofty vocation is fulfilled to the extent that the human person is able to respond to God's com-

mand with serene confidence in God's grace and in his or her own will.' On the same lines, it is part of the Church's pedagogy that husbands and wives would first recognize clearly the teaching of *Humanae Vitae* as indicating the norm for the exercise of their sexuality, and that they should endeavor to establish the conditions necessary for observing that norm" (John Paul II, Apostolic Exhortation *Familiaris Consortio*, November 22, 1981, 34).

44. "In this context, appropriate allowance is made both for *God's mercy* toward the sin of the man who experiences conversion and for the *understanding of human weakness*. Such understanding never means compromising and falsifying the standard of good and evil in order to adapt it to particular circumstances. It is quite human for the sinner to acknowledge his weakness and to ask mercy for his failings; what is unacceptable is the attitude of one who makes his own weakness the criterion of truth about the good, so that he can feel self-justified, without even the need to have recourse to God and his mercy. An attitude of this sort corrupts the morality of society as a whole, since it encourages doubt about the objectivity of the moral law in general and a rejection of the absoluteness of moral prohibitions regarding specific human acts, and it ends up by confusing all judgments about values" (John Paul II, Encyclical *Veritatis Splendor*, August 6, 1993, 104).

45. "If the confessor has no doubt about the disposition of a penitent who asks for absolution, absolution is not to be refused or delayed" (*Code of Canon Law*, can. 980).

46. "Holy Church knows full well that not infrequently, one of the parties is sinned against rather than sinning, when for a grave cause he or she reluctantly allows the perversion of the right order. In such a case, there is no sin, provided that, mindful of the law of charity, he or she does not neglect to seek to dissuade and to deter the partner from sin" (Pius XI, Encyclical *Casti Connubii, AAS* 22 (1930), 561.

47. Cf. Denzinger-Schönmetzer, *Enchiridion Symbolorum*, 2795, 3634.

48. "From the moral standpoint, it is never licit to cooperate formally in evil. Such cooperation occurs when an action, either by its

very nature or by the form it takes in a concrete situation, can be defined as a direct participation in an act against innocent human life or a sharing in the immoral intention of the person committing it" (John Paul II, Encyclical *Evangelium Vitae*, March 25, 1995, 74).

49. "Yet this discipline which is proper to the purity of married couples, far from harming conjugal love, rather confers on it a higher human value. It demands continual effort yet, thanks to its beneficent influence, husband and wife fully develop their personalities, being enriched with spiritual values. Such discipline bestows upon family life fruits of serenity and peace, and facilitates the solution of other problems; it fosters attention for one's partner, helps both parties to drive out selfishness, the enemy of true love, and deepens their sense of responsibility. By its means, parents acquire the capacity of having a deeper and more efficacious influence in the education of their offspring: little children and youths grow up with a just appraisal of human values, and in the serene and harmonious development of their spiritual and sensitive faculties" (Paul VI, Encyclical *Humanae Vitae*, July 25, 1968, 21).

50. For priests, "the first task—especially in the case of those who teach moral theology—is to expound the Church's teaching on marriage without ambiguity. Be the first to give, in the exercise of your ministry, the example of loyal internal and external obedience to the teaching authority of the Church. That obedience, as you know well, obliges not only because of the reasons adduced, but rather because of the light of the Holy Spirit, which is given in a particular way to the pastors of the Church in order that they may illustrate the truth. You know, too, that it is of the utmost importance, for peace of consciences and for the unity of the Christian people, that in the field of morals as well as in that of dogma, all should attend to the Magisterium of the Church, and all should speak the same language. Hence, with all our heart we renew to you the heartfelt plea of the great Apostle Paul: 'I appeal to you, brethren, by the name of our Lord Jesus Christ, that all of you agree and that there be no dissensions among you, but that you be united in the same mind and the same judgment.'

"To diminish in no way the saving teaching of Christ constitutes an eminent form of charity for souls. But this must ever be accompanied by patience and goodness, such as the Lord himself gave example of in dealing with men. Having come not to condemn but to save, he was indeed intransigent with evil but merciful toward individuals" (Paul VI, Encyclical *Humanae Vitae*, July 25, 1968, 28–29).

51. "With regard to the question of lawful birth regulation, the ecclesial community at the present time must take on the task of instilling conviction and offering practical help to those who wish to live out their parenthood in a truly responsible way.

"In this matter, while the Church notes with satisfaction the results achieved by scientific research aimed at more precise knowledge of the rhythms of women's fertility, and while it encourages a more decisive and wide-ranging extension of that research, it cannot fail to call with renewed vigor on the responsibility of all—doctors, experts, marriage counselors, teachers and married couples—who can actually help married people to live their love with respect for the structure and finalities of the conjugal act which expresses that love. This implies a broader, more decisive and more systematic effort to make the natural methods of regulating fertility known, respected and applied.

"A very valuable witness can and should be given by those husbands and wives who, through their joint exercise of periodic continence, have reached a more mature personal responsibility with regard to love and life. As Paul VI wrote: 'To them the Lord entrusts the task of making visible to people the holiness and sweetness of the law which unites the mutual love of husband and wife with their cooperation with the love of God the author of human life'" (John Paul II, Apostolic Exhortation *Familiaris Consortio*, November 22, 1981, 35).

52. "Since the first century the Church has affirmed the moral evil of every procured abortion. This teaching has not changed and remains unchangeable. Direct abortion, that is to say, abortion willed either as an end or a means, is gravely contrary to the moral law" (*Catechism of the Catholic Church*, 2271; see Congregation for

the Doctrine of the Faith, *Declaration on Procured Abortion*, November 18, 1974).

"The moral gravity of procured abortion is apparent in all its truth if we recognize that we are dealing with murder and, in particular when we consider the specific elements involved. The one eliminated is a human being at the very beginning of life. No one more absolutely *innocent* could be imagined" (John Paul II, Encyclical *Evangelium Vitae*, March 25, 1995, 58).

53. It is to be kept in mind that the faculty to absolve in the internal forum in this matter belongs *ipso iure*, as for all censures not reserved to the Holy See and not declared, to any bishop, even if only titular, and to the diocesan or collegiate penitentiary (can. 508), as well as to chaplains of hospitals, of prisons and of voyagers (can. 566, §2). Confessors belonging to a mendicant order or to certain modern religious congregations enjoy, by privilege, the faculty to absolve only for the censure regarding abortion.

54. Cf. John Paul II, Encyclical *Dives in Misericordia* (November 30, 1980), 14.

Appendix II

USING THIS BOOK IN THE SEMINARY

A practicum in "hearing confessions" cannot take the place of a thorough study of the history and theology of the sacrament of reconciliation. Being an effective confessor is not a matter of mastering theological principles on the one hand, or pastoral techniques on the other. Competence in both is needed. Theological expertise without sound pastoral application has little use outside of the classroom. But a pastoral practice that is not informed and guided regularly by sound theological study and reflection is dangerous. (Furthermore, as I have suggested, a priest's personal credibility as confessor is related also to his own practice as a penitent.)

Most seminary professors admit there is seldom sufficient time in any course to present adequately all that needs to be covered. This complaint certainly applies to courses on the sacrament of reconciliation. Professors realize that a seminarian's confessional practice and experience will be developed eventually "in the field," and so they usually devote class time to the sacrament's history and theology. I developed the "confessional practicum" to supplement, not to replace, these courses. The practicum attempts to help bridge the gap between what can and cannot be covered in the ordinary reconciliation course. More importantly, it provides some initial "confessional experience" while the student is in the seminary and so can benefit from guidance, supervision, and constructive criticism. I offer the following format and guidelines to my seminary colleagues who may wish to devise a practicum or confessional experience of their own.

Goals of the Course

1. to provide seminarians with some experience in hearing confessions: to familiarize them with the different ways penitents confess and the different expectations of the sacrament penitents have
2. to help seminarians develop confidence, competence, and a sense of identity in their ministry as confessor
3. to allow them to observe and learn from other "confessors"
4. to provide seminarians with an assessment of their beginning confessional practice
5. to allow them to address their "what if" and "why" questions.

Details of the Course

The practicum meets twelve times during the semester. Each session lasts about two hours. I limit class enrollment to eight students: this number allows each seminarian a number of opportunities to assume the role of confessor, and also encourages and facilitates the discussion that follows each practice confession.

Beginning the Course

After the customary introductory comments, I begin with our first practice confession. Having secured a volunteer "confessor," I assume the (stereotyped) role of a middle-aged gentleman who confesses according to the way he was taught forty years ago. I kneel behind the screen and confess—with deliberate haste—a variety of daily, "ordinary" sins. This is a confession that will be familiar to any experienced priest:

> Bless me, Father, for I have sinned. It's been about four months since my last confession. I lost my temper many times, I swore nine times, I took God's name in vain about twenty times, I lost my patience six times, I said unkind things about others ten times, I had impure thoughts six times, I didn't always pay attention at Mass four times. For these and all the sins of my past life I am truly sorry and ask for forgiveness from God and a penance and absolution from you, Father.

The above confession may be familiar to any experienced confessor, but it usually comes as a shock to the student confessor (and to his fellow students who, much to their relief, are at this point merely observers). This is likely the first confession *like this* the seminarian has heard, and it certainly isn't the well-planned, well-prepared-for sacrament of reconciliation he is accustomed to celebrating as part of his seminary formation. (Hence, the first lesson has been demonstrated well: there is much to learn!)

While this confession is different for him, in this first class session the student confessor usually tries to respond in the way his confessor responds to him. What else can he draw upon as a model or guide other than his experience? Typically, then (and not surprisingly), his sacramental dialogue seems more appropriate to a seminarian's spiritual direction session than to a fifty-year-old "preconciliar Catholic's confession." But I continue to respond in character as the (stereotyped) fifty-year-old gentleman I am role-playing. What follows is humorous only for those who have never had to experience it:

Confessor: You say you lost your temper a number of times. What causes you to do that, usually?

Penitent: I get angry. Or impatient. You know. At work, usually.

Confessor: So,...uh, you, uh, usually lose your temper at work, then?

Penitent: Yes, Father.

Confessor: Okay. Uh, yes, uh, do you sometimes lose your temper at home?

Penitent: Yes, Father.

Confessor: (Pause.) Have you, uh, thought about, uh, how you can control your temper?

Penitent: I guess so.

Confessor: Okay, good...(pause) uh, does that seem, uh, do any of those ways seem to help?

Penitent: Not really. A little, I guess.

Confessor: Good. I mean, good, uh, at least you're aware that you, uh, you need to pay attention to that.

Penitent: Pay attention to what, Father?

Confessor: Uh, your temper. I mean, why you lose your temper.

Penitent: Oh, okay, sure, Father.

It can go on like this for some time! I conclude this example by repeating verbatim the close of one of these first confessions:

Confessor: Okay. For your penance: uh, do you have a favorite scriptural passage?

Penitent: Pardon me, Father?

Confessor: Do you have, uh, do you know a passage from the scriptures that means something special to you? That, uh, is a favorite?

Penitent: A passage from...from *what*, Father?

Confessor: The scriptures. The Bible.

Penitent: Oh, yes, Father, I have a Bible, it's at home in the living room.

This first confession usually lasts no longer than five or six minutes (although the student confessor believes otherwise!). When the confession concludes, I introduce the procedure we will use throughout the semester to reflect upon and assess each practice confession. I allow the student confessor a few moments to consider what he thought about it all: what he thought about the penitent, his own words and actions, the experience. I ask him what he thought he did well, and if there was anything he would like to have the chance to do over in a different way. I then offer some comments about what the experience was like—or was likely to have been—for me, as the one confessing. Finally, his fellow seminarians have the opportunity to contribute their comments, criticisms, and suggestions. (I provide the class with copies of the chart to follow, which allows them a helpful format structure for their comments and questions.)

Subsequent Classes

For the first three class sessions or so, I arrange things so that two students can each hear two confessions. This measured pace allows ample time to discuss and ask questions, and to become familiar with the class procedure. As the semester progresses and the students become more comfortable criticizing and questioning (and acting as confessor), as many as six confessions may be heard in a single class period.

Halfway through the course, I ask three or four students to "prepare a confession" and then set aside one class period in which I play the role of confessor. I explain that my way is not necessarily the best way, and it surely is not the only way: it is, however, a more experienced way. The students recognize this willingly. The accustomed assessment and discussion follow these practice confessions—and I believe *my* ministry as confessor has benefited from this! Halfway through the semester seems to be the right point to offer them a glimpse of my "practice": by this time they have had enough initial experience, and are eager to see how one more experienced than they might approach various situations.

The "Matter" of the Confessions

Contrary to what many students initially expect, I keep potentially complicated confessions (e.g., abortion, ongoing adulterous affairs, etc.) to a minimum. Most real confessions are not particularly dramatic—which does not mean that they are not significant to the penitent or a cause of grace for priest and penitent alike. Again, the purpose of the course is not to offer them a "when this, then do this," but to help them develop a habit of listening and of considering a range of appropriate responses.

Requirements

1. I require my students to memorize the Ten Commandments and the formula for sacramental absolution. (The need to memorize the formula is obvious, and occasionally there are penitents who confess "according to the numbers." Due to the demographics in this country, I also ask my students to memorize the formula for sacramental absolution in Spanish.)

2. Each student completes a take-home essay test dealing with the material presented in the introduction to the *Rite of Penance*, the section on penance in the *Catechism of the Catholic Church* (pars. 1420–98), and Pope John Paul's *Reconciliation and Penance*. This provides the opportunity for a review of the basic theology and pastoral practice pertaining to the sacrament.

3. Each student contacts his chancery to learn the diocese's policies concerning the practice of sacramental reconciliation, including the faculties his diocese will give him upon ordination.

4. Students prepare a homily for one of several suggested communal penance services (e.g., Lenten season, high school retreat). The homily includes an examination of conscience tailored to the season or the group.

5. Towards the end of the course, each student writes a letter to his parishioners explaining what it means to him to be a confessor. (This letter encourages the seminarians to reflect further on their priestly and ministerial identity.)

6. Although not a requirement, I encourage the seminarians to address the issues of reconciliation and confession with their spiritual directors. (Again, the more comfortable and familiar with the sacrament a seminarian is as a penitent, the more comfortable and familiar he will be as confessor.)

Reading assignments include the following:

- Huels, John M. *The Pastoral Companion: A Canon Law Handbook for Catholic Ministry.* 3rd ed. rev. Quincy, IL: Franciscan Press, 2002, pp. 119–48.
- John Paul II. *Reconciliation and Penance.* (Post-Synodal Apostolic Exhortation) 2 December 1984. (Now out of print, this document may be accessed through the Holy See's website.)
- *Rite of Penance*
- *A Confessor's Handbook*

I intend to continue developing both my practicum courses in "hearing confessions" and the material I have presented in this book. I welcome comments, criticisms, and suggestions from my colleagues in the classroom, from seminarians, and from my brother priests.

(Rev.) Kurt Stasiak, O.S.B.
Saint Meinrad Seminary
St. Meinrad, IN 47577
kstasiak@saintmeinrad.edu

Assessment of the Confession Experience

1. Why was *this* penitent here? From what did this penitent need to be freed?

2. On what did the confessor seem to focus? What were his primary concerns?

3. What did the confessor seem to miss? What were the primary concerns of the penitent?

4. Was the penance assigned appropriate? Could it be "effective"? What might a "better" penance be?

5. Any questions about technique?

6. Theological questions or issues?

7. The confessor's "best moment/insight..."?

8. The confessor's "mistakes/lapses..."?

9. Finally, what is the most important thing *you* learned from observing (or hearing) this confession?

Appendix III

"Confessors Need to Be Penitents, Too"[1]

The sacrament of reconciliation holds a curious place in the lives of priests. Ask any of us to recall the particularly significant moments of our ministry, for example, and the chances are good that, whether we've been ordained five years or fifty, we'll speak first—and we'll speak often—of our ministry as confessor.

But there is another side to the experience many priests have with the sacrament. Ask us how often we celebrate the sacrament *as the one confessing.* "Infrequently." "Seldom." "Well, it's been a while." I hear these answers regularly. I hear them more than I think I should.

Why this paradox? Why is a sacrament we readily acknowledge to be such a powerful and beautiful part of our ministry also a sacrament a number of us hesitate to approach from "the other side of the screen"?

Pope John Paul II believes priests must take advantage of the sacrament they minister to others. He remarks that when they do not, their relationships with their parishioners, with their bishop and brother priests, and with God "suffer an inexorable decline." Priests neglect the sacrament, the Pope says, not only at the expense of their ministry but also of their "*priestly being*"—the whole of their priestly existence.

Furthermore, Pope John Paul suggests that priests must be regular and faithful "confessees" *in order to be truly effective confessors:*

But I also add that even in order to be a good and effective minister of Penance the priest needs to have recourse to the source of grace and holiness present in this Sacrament. We priests, on the basis of our personal experience, can certainly say that, the more careful we are to receive the Sacrament of Penance and to approach it frequently and with good dispositions, the better we fulfill our own ministry as confessors and ensure that our penitents benefit from it. And on the other hand, this ministry would lose much of this effectiveness if in some way we were to stop being good penitents. Such is *the internal logic* of this great Sacrament. It invites all of us priests of Christ to pay renewed attention to our personal confession.[2]

Pope John Paul maintains that the "internal logic" of the sacrament demands that good ministers be regular penitents. But the logic is not always followed, nor is the ideal always pursued. And so while this sacrament is a treasure trove of resources for forming and nourishing the spiritual lives of priests, it seems as though it is a treasure often left buried in a field—mostly forgotten, if not altogether ignored.

The Church's dogmatic teaching on the sacrament stresses the forgiveness of sins and the conferral of sanctifying grace. Acknowledging these effects of the sacrament, I wish to explore other values—other treasures—the regular reception of the sacrament can offer us. These are treasures we may not always or immediately consider when we think of "going to confession." But I believe they are treasures too important for our priestly ministry (indeed, as John Paul II has suggested, too essential for our *priestly being*) to leave them buried and unused. What "regular reception" of the sacrament means is part of almost any discussion of the sacrament today. To encourage that discussion among my brother priests—perhaps even to start an argument!—I propose that *celebrating the sacrament as a "confessee" regularly means, for priests, cele-brating it no less than six times a year.*[3]

1. Accountability

Essential to the genuine celebration of the sacrament of rec-onciliation (and to all human growth) is the notion of accountability. Examining our conscience; reflecting upon the harm done or the good left undone; resolving to repair and to amend: this kind of accountability, this *taking account of and for our lives,* has always been the first step in celebrating the sacrament, whatever its various forms in our Church's history.

Certainly, sacramental reconciliation calls all Christians to account for the grace and obligations of their baptism. But for us priests, because of who we are—because of who we have publicly said we want to be—this call to accountability is all the more compelling.

We are fortunate in that our sins usually are known to us alone. But whether others know of our sins misses the point. One promise we made at our ordination—and one obligation we accepted—was that our private and our public lives would bear witness to each other. We promised that the person we are in public and the person we are in private would comple-ment and support, and not contradict or weaken, each other. As a priest friend of mine says often: "A priest is entitled to a private life—but not a secret one."

There are two moments in the rite of ordination to the dia-conate when these promises and obligations of consistency and accountability are given special mention. At the beginning of the ordination rite, the bishop reminds the deacon candi-dates of the practical implications of their being set apart:

[N]ow you must not only listen to God's word but also preach it. Hold the mystery of faith with a clear conscience. Express in action what you proclaim by word of mouth.[4]

Later in the rite, as he presents the new deacons with the Book of the Gospels, the bishop again spells out the implications of their new ministry:

Receive the Gospel of Christ,
whose herald you now are.
Believe what you read,
teach what you believe,
and practice what you teach.[5]

As priests, we hold a position in our Church that *is essentially different* than those we serve. One part of this essential difference stems from our *public* promise of commitment both to a life of *public* ministry in our Church (the priest as apostle) and to a life of continual *interior* conversion and growth in Christ (the priest as disciple).[6] Yes, all Christians are called to be apostles and disciples. But we have accepted the burden—we have promised others we want to be seen as accepting the burden—of committing our lives to these two "Christian preoccupations." If our priestly ministry is not just a job that "really anybody could do," it is because we want there to be a striking consistency between the public and professional works of our hands and the private and personal thoughts of our heart.

Because we are priests, our way of life must be different. Or, perhaps better, *we are priests because we want our way of life to be different.* Again, the distinction speaks not to an alleged greater state of holiness, but to a witness consistent with the internal reality of Orders and the visible status of service and witness Orders offers the Church. We serve neither ourselves nor others well when we blur this distinction by bowing to the demands of a superficial egalitarianism or accommodating a thoughtless political correctness. As Father Raymond Brown has pointed out: "A God who is not holier than the world is otiose; and similarly a priesthood that does not stand apart in some way is a priesthood that is not needed."[7]

Now you must not only listen to God's word but also preach it....Practice what you teach. There is nothing private about being a Christian. Christians receive the light of Christ through their baptism and, as the gospel says, "No one lights a lamp and then hides it under a basket." If all Christians are called to be a light to the world, those ordained to serve are called all the more. Rightly setting aside distinctions of holiness, we cannot blur the distinctions of service and leadership. Again, the gospel: "The one to whom much has been entrusted, even more will be demanded." And, again, Father Brown has put it succinctly: "If Christians are called upon to be a light to the world, it has been thought that priests are called upon to be a light to the Christian community."[8]

We have accepted the call to be "special lights to the Christian community." We are the sparks that constantly ignite and keep alive the light of the Christian community so it may burn for all to see. The sacrament is a call to accountability: a call to honesty and integrity. While we must never think ourselves better than those whom we are ordained to serve—and while we must not consider ourselves members of a privileged elite—we must remember we are "set apart" and so are "different" than those we serve. *We must be different for their sake.* The call to accountability the sacrament of reconciliation offers us can assist us in not taking the "lowest common denominator" approach to ourselves as ministers or our conversion as priests. As we answer the call to be public ministers of, to, and for the Church, the sacrament challenges us to take account of our lives in the light of those calls.

2. A *Return to Grace*

God, our *Father*. We, his *children*. These ways of thinking about God and ourselves came naturally to us when we *were* children. Perhaps we even began our prayer with that charming cuteness only a child can master: "Dear Daddy, who art in heaven."

As adults we long ago abandoned cuteness in our prayer (and often charm in our lives!). And perhaps we've also lost our appreciation of the profound reality those "childhood images" speak of: God, our *Father*. We, God's *children*. Rather than being a measure of adult maturity, this loss would seem to be an adult's road to peril. For it was a child Jesus took in his arms and said, "It is to such as these that the kingdom of God belongs." On another occasion, Jesus even warned his disciples, "Unless you become like this child, you will not enter the Kingdom of God."

What is it about children that has Jesus describing them as those "to whom the Kingdom belongs"? It is not their cuteness, it is not their innocence. Nor is it what these children will one day be able to accomplish or achieve. What seems to establish them as the privileged inheritors of the Kingdom is that children are, by nature, *dependent*. They look to another for life, for food, for love—for their identity. And children do this naturally, even willingly. They seem to have little difficulty asking those "bigger than they" for what they need.

We teach well when we explain that the sacraments encourage—indeed, demand—our response to be truly fruitful. And we are correct in frowning on any approach that suggests sacraments "work" as long as the "rite is right." Grace is a gift, but a gift must be unwrapped to be used.

In our efforts to unwrap the gift God gives us, however, we can become too impressed with *our* skills, *our* talents, *our* knowledge and insights. In short, we are seduced by what *we* have done. Many reasons are offered to explain the diminishing numbers of Catholics approaching the sacrament of reconciliation today. "Catholics are more sophisticated, more mature, more *adult*," we often hear. But as we have acquired a greater adult Christian maturity, have we lost a sense of basic Christian *humility*?

Humility is not humiliation. Humility is the experience that leads to and encourages the fundamental Christian attitude, that of *thankfulness*. Those who are truly humble are humble because they know their gifts *as gifts*. And because they know this, they cannot be other than thankful.

Here, the sacrament of reconciliation offers us an opportunity to "return to grace"—specifically, to return to the grace of our baptism, when God adopted us as his children. We grow in years and stature and maybe even in wisdom. But we remain always *children* of God. When we forget this, we sin. And it is easy to forget this. Most often, we forget it because we do not remember to give thanks.

We forget when we are complimented and do not thank the One through whom all good things come. We forget when we applaud ourselves on our growth and do not remember those who have been effective instruments of God's grace to us in that growth. We forget when, perhaps most often, we just don't remember to remember God. Pope John Paul remarks that this forgetting was the sin of the tower builders of Babel, *a sin "presented not so much under the aspect of opposition to [God] as of forgetfulness and indifference towards him, as if God were of no relevance in the sphere of man's joint projects."*[9]

Doing good things without including God in our plans is not a sin specific to priests. But it may be one of *our* greatest temptations. The tower builders of Babel ultimately failed because:

> they had set up as a sign and guarantee of the unity they desired a work of their own hands alone, and had forgotten the action of the Lord. They had attended only to the horizontal dimension of work and social life, forgetting the vertical dimension by which they would have been rooted in God, their Creator and Lord, and would have been directed towards him as the ultimate goal of their progress.[10]

God does not rely upon the sacraments to forgive our sins or offer us his grace. We need the sacraments, however, to remind ourselves that forgiveness is grace and gift. God's love is not something we earn, nor is God's forgiveness a reward for our good intentions. As Weekday Preface IV reminds us: "You have no need of our praise, yet our desire to thank you is itself your gift." This awareness is as old as Christianity itself: "For by grace you have been saved through faith, and this is not your own doing; it is the gift of God—not the result of works, so that no one may boast" (Eph 2:8–9).

Reconciliation is an occasion when God's offer of grace is made particularly manifest. It is also a time when our response of gratitude can be clearly expressed. Our confession is not merely the acknowledgment of our sins, but is also our "confession"—our acknowledgment, our remembering—of God's loving mercy. And we need to take the time to say "thank you," just as we need times *when we cannot escape saying those words.* For not to say thank you is to risk forgetting that we have reason to give thanks. Not to be thankful is to risk forgetting what Christians must never forget: that they owe a debt to Another. As one writer has suggested, it is significant that one of the first things parents teach their children to say is "thank you":

To be a child means to owe one's existence to another, and even in our adult life we never quite reach the point where we no longer have to give thanks for being the person we are. This means that we never quite outgrow our condition of children, nor do we therefore ever outgrow the obligation to give thanks for ourselves or to continue to ask for our being. Individual men, cultures and institutions may forget this. Only the Christian religion, which in its essence is communicated by the eternal child of God, keeps alive in its believers the lifelong awareness of their being children, and therefore of having to ask and give thanks for things. *Jesus does not insist on this childlike "say please", "say thank you", because otherwise the gifts would be refused, but in order that they may be recognized as gifts.*[11]

One value of the sacrament of reconciliation is that we remind ourselves of our sinfulness. Perhaps an even greater value—a greater treasure we need to unbury—is developing the habit of giving thanks for the gift of God's grace, and so continue to recover our relationship as one of his children: one of those "to whom the Kingdom belongs."

3. Being a minister of reconciliation "in and out of season"

I am interested in exploring how the sacrament of reconciliation can form and shape our life—*all* our life, *all the time*. Again, I believe we are priests because we want our way of life to be different.

We despise being thought of as liturgical functionaries, as "sacramental robots" who enter, do ritual, and then depart. We see our role as priest as extending beyond the liturgical celebration of the sacraments. We consider priesthood a way of life, not an opportunity for employment. And there, precisely, is the challenge. How, exactly, have we embraced our priesthood? Better yet, how have we allowed our priesthood to embrace us?

Specifically, to what extent have we appropriated the title "minister of reconciliation" into our "personal" lives? To refer to our first point above, how *accountable* are we to our ministry of reconciliation when we hang up our stole, walk away from the confessional, and again rub shoulders with our peers, our parishioners, with people of all sorts? Reflecting upon this can be painful, as the following example demonstrates.

I had been criticizing a coworker. My criticisms reflected the usual inventory of annoyances we experience living and working with others. I had criticized this person before, without really thinking about it. Without really thinking about it, I would probably do so again.

A short time later he was in my office. But now our relationship was different. My coworker was not coming to me as a colleague. He was coming to me now because, in his eyes, he was a sinner. And he was coming to *me* because, in his eyes, I was a priest: a person of compassion and understanding, a sacramental minister of God's forgiveness.

He confessed some of the very things I had been criticizing him for only a short time before. A strange feeling: what I heard him confess I already knew! What I was hearing for the first time, however, was how *he* saw himself. I heard him acknowledging his faults. I heard him talk about how he tried to deal with them. I listened to him talk about his efforts— and his fears and frustrations.

More significant than what I was hearing, however, was what I was feeling—also, embarrassingly, for the first time. Listening to him, "seeing him" admit his sins, I felt some of the pain he so often felt in knowing he was the butt of many jokes and the subject of frequent criticism.

Seldom have I been so determined to be an ambassador of God's peace to a penitent as I was then. What was haunting me at the time—what has haunted me since—was seeing this person, a person who not too long ago had been the object of my ill will, now approach me as the *minister* of the Church's sacrament of reconciliation. I realized then that however competent or effective I might be as a sacramental minister of reconciliation, my being a reconciling person remained on the "professional" level. As far as this person was concerned, I had yet to appropriate my professional ministry into my "personal" life.

Hypocrisy? I pray that God will not judge hypocritical my contributing to this person's pain before being his sacramental minister of peace. To be human is to be sinfully inconsistent. Perhaps the word *hypocrite* refers more to those who, confronted with their sinful inconsistency, acknowledge it *but do not care.*

But perhaps there is nothing more *paradoxical* than a priest who criticizes rather than accepts, who hurts rather than heals, and whose words—whenever, wherever they are spoken—contribute to the common gossip rather than promote the common good. The paradox is obvious. As priests, we see a lot of what most people see only a little. We see how people suffer, we see their pain, and we see them struggling—often heroically and with scant resources—to do the good they want to do and avoid the evil they want to avoid. We have seen these things, these people, and so should we not take extraordinary care to be Christ's ambassadors of peace "in season and out of season"? Outside the confessional as well as within it?

I had a second experience with the sacrament later that day—this time from "the other side." In the first experience, that with my colleague, I hope that I helped heal a wound and ease some pain, as I called upon the power of God's grace to supply what was lacking in human efforts. In the second experience, that with *my* confessor, my hopes and prayers were similar.

And I prayed to remember that the compassion and understanding I offer others as confessor is a compassion and understanding that I can—*and that I must*—try to offer no matter the occasion, the situation, or the person.

4. Practice Towards Becoming an Effective Confessor

I believe we priests need to practice continually becoming an effective confessor. This is not to suggest that we should celebrate the sacrament as penitents so that we will learn something about "how to hear" confessions. That *will* happen, of course, naturally and inevitably. Just as teachers usually begin teaching according to the way they were taught in the classroom, so do we offer spiritual direction and hear confessions (at least at the beginning) along the lines of how we have been directed or confessed.

When I propose that our "going to confession" is a practice towards becoming an effective minister of the sacrament, I mean "practice" in the same way that our prayer is a practice for our ministry or that our reflection upon the scriptures is a practice for our preaching. Talking daily with God; regular study of the scriptures; approaching the sacrament as penitent: these are practices for our priesthood because *they direct and strengthen our relationship with the God whom we seek and whom we strive to serve.*

Becoming an effective homilist, for example, involves more than mastering the intricacies of exegesis or the skills of public speaking. The homilist who truly inspires—the priest who really *breathes* God's Spirit into people—surely benefits from studying some commentaries and practicing his delivery.

These professional competencies are, however, means to an end. The truly effective homilist is effective not so much because of his professional competence but because of his personal credibility. He is credible because he *knows* what is going on in the scripture passage. He speaks "with authority" about what happens as Jesus and people encounter each other because he has experienced that interaction in his own life.

Similarly, becoming an effective confessor involves more than learning psychological theory or counseling techniques. The truly effective confessor is the credible confessor. He is credible because he knows the fear and courage with which his people approach the sacrament. He is credible because he has experienced, with another minister, both the embarrassment of his sin and, through another, has experienced the gift of God's grace. Whatever he knows about human behavior or the art of counseling will help him help his penitents. But he will continue becoming an effective confessor to the degree that he knows what it is to confess to another and have another minister to him. Often professional competence will support and strengthen our personal credibility. Seldom can professional competence *replace* our personal credibility.

To confess to another is not an easy task, either for parishioner or for priest. We approach the sacrament because we have offended others. We confess because at times we choose, foolishly, forgetfully, moments of death rather than life. We need to be penitents because we need to say aloud and to another—we need to say to our Church—that we are sorry and that we know we are in debt to Another. But these are not easy things to do. These attitudes are not easy to adopt and maintain.

Still, great treasures are worth the effort it takes to dig them out, pull them up and, perhaps, even ask for some help in prying open the lid. I have suggested that, as the sacrament of reconciliation is an indispensable part in the life of every Christian, it can be an especially tremendous treasure of grace in the lives of us priests. We, who have accepted the responsibility of hearing God's word and proclaiming it, need to take account of our faithfulness to that responsibility. We, the stewards of God's grace to our people through our sacramental ministry, need to return to that grace ourselves in thanksgiving and in humility. We, who so often see firsthand the hopes and the horrors of the heart, need to allow our ministry as reconcilers to direct how we act outside of the confessional as well as within it. And we, who offer God's pardon and peace to others, know those gifts best when we have heard those words of absolution offered for us, to us.

To paraphrase the words of Pope John Paul: when we priests do take advantage of the sacrament we offer to others, it is not only our priestly ministry that benefits but our priestly being, *the whole of our priestly existence*. With so much at stake, the sacrament of reconciliation for priests—from "both sides of the screen"—is too great a treasure to leave buried in a field.

Notes to Appendix III

1. The material in Appendix III is reworked slightly from my article, "Reconciliation for Priests," *Priest* (February 1999), 12–18, and is reprinted here with the permission of *Priest*.

2. John Paul II, *Reconciliation and Penance* (Post-Synodal Apostolic Exhortation, 2 Dec. 1984), par. 31–VI; emphasis in original.

3. Some will consider this woefully infrequent. Others will consider it excessive. Let the arguments begin!

4. Rite of Ordination of Deacons 14 (Bishop's homily to the deacons-elect).

5. Rite of Ordination of Deacons 24 (Presentation of the Book of the Gospels).

6. I rely here upon Raymond Brown's fine reflection on these models in his *Priest and Bishop: Some Biblical Reflections* (New York: Paulist Press, 1970), 21–34.

7. Brown, *Priest and Bishop,* 9.

8. Brown, *Priest and Bishop,* 22.

9. Pope John Paul II, *Reconciliation and Penance,* par. 14; emphasis mine.

10. Pope John Paul II, *Reconciliation and Penance,* par. 13.

11. Hans Urs von Balthasar, *Unless You Become Like This Child,* trans. Erasmo Leiva-Merikakis (San Francisco: Ignatius, 1991), 49–50; emphasis mine.

ABOUT THE WORKS CITED

Broccolo, Gerard T. "The Minister of Penance" in *The New Rite of Penance: Background Catechesis*. St. Piux X Abbey, Pevely, MO: F.D.L.C., 1975, pp. 50–64. Also appears as *Ten Characteristics of the Presidential Style of a Good Confessor*. Chicago: Liturgy Training Program, 1975. (Although written a quarter-century ago, Broccolo's essay continues to offer challenging models upon which confessors can reflect and so assess their sacramental ministry.)

Coffey, David M. *The Sacrament of Reconciliation* (*Lex Orandi* series. John D. Laurance, series editor). Collegeville: Liturgical Press, 2001. (A study of the theology of the sacrament, based primarily on the postconciliar rite of reconciliation.)

Häring, Bernard. *Shalom: Peace; the Sacrament of Reconciliation*. Garden City, NY: Image, 1969. (Forty years old, this book is out of print, but copies may still be available from various websites. Fr. Häring's reflections on the sacrament from both the moral and pastoral perspectives are worth the effort in acquiring this book.)

John Paul II. *Reconciliation and Penance*. Post-Synodal Apostolic Exhortation. 2 December 1984. (A major papal statement on humankind's need to "reconcile and be reconciled." Parts One and Two offer an extensive reflection on conversion, reconciliation, and the mysteries of sin and forgiveness. Part Three reviews Church teaching on the sacrament of reconciliation, and offers Pope John Paul's insights and directives concerning its pastoral practice.)

Pontifical Council for the Family. *Vademecum for Confessors Concerning Some Aspects of the Morality of Conjugal Life*. 12 February 1997. (Included as Appendix I of this book, this "companion for confessors" provides priests with a helpful context and with pastoral suggestions for their ministry to married penitents.)

Rahner, Karl. "The Meaning of Frequent Confession of Devotion" in *Theological Investigations III*. New York: Seabury, 1967, pp. 177–89. (In addition to discussing the practice of "devotional confessions," Father Rahner offers insight into the unique nature and value of the forgiveness of sins *through the sacrament*.)

———. "Problems Concerning Confession" in *Theological Investigations III*, pp. 190–206. (Father Rahner reports problematic trends and attitudes associated with sacramental reconciliation, and discusses how a better understanding of this sacrament can increase its value in the lives of priests and parishioners alike.)

———. "Guilt and its Remission: the Borderland between Theology and Psychotherapy" in *Theological Investigations II*. Baltimore: Helicon, 1963, pp. 265–81. (This essay addresses the distinctive nature of sacramental reconciliation in light of the increasing popularity and availability of secular and "professional" techniques of healing.)

United States Catholic Conference. *Reflections on the Sacrament of Penance in Catholic Life Today: A Study Document*, Washington, DC: U.S.C.C., Inc., 1990. (This study reports the attitudes and habits American priests and parishioners bring to the sacrament of reconciliation, and offers practical recommendations concerning the sacrament's catechesis and celebration.)